Shifts

Shifts is full of humor and truth and completely relatable for any stage of the womanhood journey. The experiences shared by this wide range of women provides a source of strength and inspiration.

Leah T. Johnson
Co-Founder and Editor, *ColorBlind* Magazine

Life is full of transitions – some subtle, some earth-shattering. You may be a suburban stay-at-home mom holding your marriage together for appearance's sake, an immigrant coming to grips with the nuances of the English language within the context of the American culture or a cancer survivor adjusting to your "new normal." Regardless of your circumstances, Shifts *will give you an "a-ha" moment on every page.*

Valerie F. Leonard
Expert, Community and Organizational Development, Chicago, IL

All too often, we tend to think that women only experience change as it relates to menarche and its cessation. Shifts: An Anthology of Women's Growth Through Change *highlights a variety of transfigurations contemporary American women experience throughout their life cycles, particularly changes in identity associated with adolescence, mothering, immigration, economic instability, and the stigma of old age. Although their voices and circumstances differ, each woman's story underscores how such challenges can be met with courage, resilience, and inner strength.*

Kathleen Renk, Ph.D.
Professor of English, Northern Illinois University, Dekalb, IL
Author of *Caribbean Shadows and Victorian Ghosts: Women's Writing and Decolonization* (University Press of Virginia)

I admire the editors for so boldly taking on the angst-riddled journeys of women. Each entry is uniquely woven and honestly depicts the struggle of evolution when staying stagnant is no doubt the easier path. A fascinating exploration of the discovery of strength, often times in the most unexpected places.

Tarvis Thompson
Publicist/Communications Executive, Atlanta, GA

Shifts

An Anthology of Women's Growth Through Change

Edited by Michelle Duster and Trina Sotira

with Jen Cullerton Johnson

*Muse*Write
PRESS

Copyright © 2015 by MuseWrite Press
P.O. Box 19550, Chicago, IL 60619
www.musewrite.com

Library of Congress Control Number: 2014921558
ISBN 978-0-9899609-1-5

First Edition: Second Printing

Copy Editor   Debra Almgren-Horwitz
Cover design by Robin Ludwig Designs
Cover photo "Glass Window Bridge" by Sheree Nielsen

In memory of my great-grandmothers and grandmothers who endured many injustices but never gave up their dignity. In honor of my mother, aunts, cousins, friends and mentors who taught me that you should never make yourself small in order to make someone else feel big.

– MD

For the women who were fueled by courage to tell their stories, and for my fearless leader, Bonnie Bradstreet.

– TS

For Colleen Cullerton Liddy. Love Always.

– JCJ

CONTENTS

SELF-RESPECT

SELF-ACCEPTANCE

SELF-DISCOVERY

SELF-WORTH

❖

INTRODUCTION

Every morning on my drive to campus, I pass through downtown Glen Ellyn, Illinois decorated with small shops and coffee houses. A train depot houses commuters; a bus stop lures riders. If I am early enough, I drive through town just as the homeless are let out of the local shelters and churches. If I am early enough, I have just enough time to have my heart broken by the number of women I find strolling the streets with their parcels dragging behind them on wired carts. One morning, I was early enough to find a woman dressed in an old tweed coat and a stitched cap, her hand pressed against the window of a high-end boutique. She stared at the outfit as long as the train stopped to take passengers. While people piled in the train across the street, she kept her gaze on the dress-pants and shirt, leather purse and heels. Glass separated this woman from touching the clothing. But what was so crushing about this moment was I knew she had a story. I knew she didn't choose to be on the streets, didn't choose to gaze at beautiful things with the dying heart of want and need and things she could not obtain. Something brought her there. Something stopped her from obtaining her dreams, goals, and moments when she'd have the opportunity to wear an outfit in a window. I knew she had a story.

Like many of the pieces in *Shifts*, all women are united by their stories. Michelle Cliff's Caribbean novel *Abeng* reminds us that stories preserve lives. Shared narratives not only create a dialogue about women's issues, but they also provide validation that, in turn, can create value. If we must quantify life, then perhaps we can calculate the value of our lives by the stories we share. After all, our legacies are preserved through the words we choose to tell our tales.

We don't reflect on the deceased commenting on how much money they had or what kind of countertops sparkled in their kitchens; rather, we remember a story about them. When children's book writer and friend Laura Crawford passed away last year, a group of eight writers met after her wake and shared stories. We laughed and cried in her memory. And I knew her forty-something years on earth were well-spent simply by the stories we told. In this anthology, we have pulled together to share our stories to preserve our lives.

Writers from across the globe, from college professors to celebrated authors, award-winning poets to anthologized essayists, have joined on the page to preserve our struggles and our celebrations. And some of the stories are heartbreaking, sharing the pain of loss from terrorizing miscarriages to children vacating homes for college. Some are celebratory, epiphanies and moments of strength. And some are hidden secrets, where one of the authors has broken open a wound, ready to finally share the story with others. We can almost picture some of the writers cupping their hands to lips, whispering their story in our ears. Whether it's a whisper or a shout, we hope you find yourself reading one of the essays, poems, or short stories, shaking your head in agreement, recognizing the narratives that unite us. We hope that the conversation continues from this anthology into living rooms and through telephones, moving from muffled voices to magnified discussions. Like an ear to a shell, hearing the waves as an echo of your own lifeline, we hope you cup your hand and hear the words of your life speak from the pages of this book.

    – Trina Sotira

Eavesdropping

Kara Provost

The grownups talk in the other room —
two worlds divided by a door —
if we come through they'll fall silent,
then ask: *What do you want?*

We want, don't want to hear their talk,
eavesdropping, half-afraid of what we'll find,
like heaving up a rock
to expose a skittering crab.

We want, don't want to be let in
to that world in the other room
where they sip bitter black coffee
or drinks in tall glasses with ice and odd names.

Where they read newspapers, endless
columns of black and white
and small, small letters, listen
to music with no words.

Maybe we'll stay
on this side of the door
overhearing, spying, deciding
if those secrets are worth growing up for.

SELF-RESPECT

Introducing the New Auntie M
MK Miller

As soon as my little sister announced her pregnancy, I descended onto parental how-to guides with a vengeance—*What To Expect When You're Expecting, What to Expect the First Year, The Hip Mama Survival Guide,* you name it. And then there are the purchases—to date, this includes: five storybooks, a set of yellow hair bows, a pair of red polka-dot sunglasses (girls need accessories!), and one deliciously flouncy pink dress—and that's before the baby shower crib I kicked in for.

Never mind that I've not—and probably never will—have a child. Is this faux-nesting behavior just this side of a doting auntie-to-be?

Even during events that were focused on work, I was obsessed with the impending foray of auntdom. While attending a conference, a group of coworkers and I decided after dinner and a drink or three, to visit a psychic.

I expected little or nothing from my professed clairvoyant, but I'd barely gotten my backside onto the chair when the psychic congratulated me on "your little sister's pregnancy," called the baby a girl, and told me the first letter of her given name would be W. She then pronounced my unmitigated excitement about the child—all true and I'd uttered not a peep.

My heart skidded.

"Your excitement has to do with another lifetime." *Of course,* I winced. *Doesn't it always?*

The psychic went on to describe a scenario involving the Deep South, a top-hatted husband and me in a carriage, followed by weeping in a parlor. In the coffin were the bodies of a woman and infant draped together. Even if it was illogical, as a woman with a perpetual soft spot in my heart for Southern literature and melancholy, her historical explanation pleased me immensely.

"This is your second chance," the psychic without-aid-of-magic-ball explained. "It's why you have three times the happiness of a regular auntie about the birth of this child, since you were denied the experience then."

She *did* have a point there. My enthusiasm has been oddly off-the-charts. I had already perused good birthday party venues and a relative might have gently suggested waiting a few years to stock my niece's library with *Junie B. Jones* and *Little Women*.

Why do I want to be so involved? I couldn't stop wondering. Why *am* I so eager about my impending auntdom?

Is it that, as a single woman, I have so much expendable income? Hardly—I still carry last decade's student debt and the life of an artist has "padded" my bank balance straight to a requisite day job. My brother-in-law consistently nets numerous times my salary in commissions on a "slow" year.

While I'm close to my sister, I can't imagine she'd be so generous with presents or zeal if the situations were reversed. In fact, while she's taking excellent care of my niece in utero, I've consistently waxed more enthusiastic about Willa Belle's arrival than my morning-sick queasy sibling.

Could this be the joy of auntiehood? No stretch marks. No stretching, retching over a toilet all hours of day or night. No leaky breasts or midnight feedings.

Granted, depictions of aunties have been a mixed bag. The sedate mother substitute, like Auntie Em in *The Wizard of Oz,* is hardly a person to get excited about, nor is the white-haired widow or the old maid akin to Tweety Bird's bun-haired, knitting bag-wielding protectress. I don't see myself in such portrayals. My hair has been Sleek Sable for over ten years thanks to my excellent colorist. And my ability to make things was proven to be fantasy when my sole foray into sewing in home economics was such a fiasco that my teacher volunteered to finish the final stitches herself. I'm convinced that the only mother I'm likely to be mistaken for is of the fairy variety.

Could it be that I aim to live vicariously through my sister's parental experiences? Possibly. In my mid-thirties, most of my high school friends already have tweens (if not teens). The majority of my college friends and cousins have elementary schoolers and I get to take part in story reading, birthday and pool parties, and parent-date-night babysitting to my heart's content. While the frivolity of spending formative moments with these children has been precious, I've also been given a glimpse into how exhausting parenthood can be by watching my friends lead lives filled with shuffling children from one place to the next. Their adorable little offspring have caused my harried friends to create color-coded schedules all over refrigerators, even before preschool and t-ball begin.

I don't know if I ever had or ever will have the stamina to raise a child. Most days my West Highland Terrier keeps me plenty busy. I always knew that I wanted to be a writer with the fervor that most girls attribute to their wedding day fantasies and naming their future babies. My plans always worked towards pen, ink, and publication. But does that mean I have to forego being instrumental in children's lives?

Happily, I'm on the cusp of a growing trend of over-the-moon aunties. According to the 2010 US census, 47.1 percent of women

15-44, don't have kids. Within my age range—35-39—I was surprised to learn that the figure is still a relatively high 19.7 percent. Can it be that one in five of us is available to cuddle, educate, amuse, and otherwise adore the children in our midst? Melanie Notkin of Savvy Auntie.com has coined an appropriate acronym: PANK (Professional Aunt No Kids). Color me PANK— and proud! If, famously, it takes a village to raise a child, then today's PANKS are America's great unrecognized and untapped resource.

"Your niece," the psychic concluded, "wants me to tell you that she's going to love and admire her auntie very much."

Isn't that the point entirely? Aunties give and receive reciprocal investments of love, admiration, and emotional connection. Nurturing Willa Belle is sure to be the most ongoing, longest-flourishing relationship of my adult life. I get to remain an independent entity while also letting her know that I'm her forever ally. What's not to adore about such an arrangement?

The Only Poem
Hannah Cook Cross

Before, love was a straight line.
Or maybe a line segment drawn taut,
point A to point B.
Now it is circular, spiral, ovular,
        centripetal.

He grew from a tiny bud in me, a hope
given up on suddenly thriving.
So careful to preserve the arrow of his life:
        no drink   no secondhand smoke   no chemicals
In utero, he was torture:
sickness, blinding headaches
        nodrivingnoliftingnocaffeinenosex

Then: birth.

I had to learn to feed him from my own body,
learn to love him as my own soul,
only separate.
Two points on the same closed time-like curve.

So much hope, so many expectations: to love to shape to influence
to control a
finished product

all love,
scold to keep safe, gently correct
bad manners

Perhaps I can influence
reactions, attitudes

but I cannot change
the core of what God made him, his
immutable self.

I can only listen as
he tells me who he is.
His will is strong, stronger
than mine.
I can refine, distill, guide.

I was, and he is.
Now I am
we.

A Modern Woman Visits Her Brother's Wife

Elizabeth Gauffreau

From time to time, Livy would get an invitation from Velma, hand written on her personalized blue stationery and mailed, to join her for dessert. Livy would accept with a telephone call, and when she arrived on the appointed evening, it would be just Velma and her, Walter off to a meeting of one of the civic organizations he had recently joined. Velma seemed to take such pleasure in presenting Livy with coconut cake and lemon meringue pie and chocolate ice cream and once even Baked Alaska that Livy had to wonder if Velma had enough to do all day. However, she hesitated to ask Velma such a question so soon after her marriage.

Livy refrained from asking the question for months. Then one hot summer night she found herself on Velma's sun porch with a dish of hand-churned vanilla ice cream in front of her and a gingersnap in her hand, cookie crisp and perfect despite the humid day, and the thought occurred to her that it had probably taken Velma more than one try to get the gingersnaps right.

Livy pointed at the plate. "How many batches did you make before you got these to come out right?"

"What?" Velma said, then quickly, "Pardon?"

"These gingersnaps," Livy said, gesturing with the one still in her hand. "It's been beastly humid all week. These couldn't have come out right the first time."

"They didn't," Velma said.

"And you made them again."

"Yes, I did."

"You shouldn't do that," Livy said.

Velma did not answer her, grimly holding a glass of iced tea in her hand.

"Aren't there other things you'd rather be doing?" Livy said.

Velma brought the glass to her lips and drank from it before answering. "Of course there are."

She did not elaborate, and Livy let the matter drop, vowing to return to it the next time she was invited for dessert.

It was over two months later and well into an unusually wet autumn before Livy received another invitation. She walked to Walter's house in the rain, having made up her mind that she would talk to Velma, the thought never occurring to her that perhaps she should talk to her brother instead.

When Livy arrived at the house, the outside light had not been turned on, nor had the light in the foyer, the only light in the house coming from a single bridge lamp in the living room. Livy lifted the doorknocker and wondered if Velma had forgotten her invitation; perhaps she and Walter had gone out together.

Livy knocked again and was peering through the sidelight next to the door when footsteps sounded across the floor and the door opened. Velma leaned forward to push open the storm door. "Come in out of the rain, Livy. You're soaking wet."

Livy set her umbrella in the umbrella stand next to the door and hung her coat in the hall closet while Velma stood and watched. As Livy stood on the rug in the middle of the foyer shaking out her hair, Velma turned away. Livy followed her into the living room and sat in the Morris chair next to the fireplace. From time to time, a drop of rain fell down the chimney and onto the cold ashes of a recent evening fire, sending out a strong, unpleasant burned smell.

Velma remained standing by the front window, her face reflected dimly in the dark glass. Her face looked odd, as though the features had somehow gone out of alignment, the hazel eyes closer together, the small mouth adrift between the pale cheeks.

"I'm sorry," Velma said, after some minutes had passed. "Your dessert isn't ready."

"That's all right," Livy said. "I came here to see you."

"I was going to serve angel food cake with an orange glaze," Velma said. "I made the cake, but the oranges were hard to peel." She turned back to the window.

"That's all right," Livy repeated. She stood up and crossed the room to where Velma was standing. "What's wrong?" She put her hand on Velma's shoulder and asked again, what's wrong?, but when Velma flinched, Livy took her hand away.

"I don't know," Velma said without looking at her.

"Look," Livy said, "why don't I make us some tea? We can sit in the kitchen. I think you've been watching the rain too long."

"I've been watching the rain all afternoon," Velma said and followed Livy into the kitchen, sitting down at the white enameled table and watching Livy pull open drawers and poke into cupboards without getting up to stop her. She even let Livy open the door of her new Frigidaire.

Livy found everything she needed for the tea, laid it out, and put the kettle on. While she waited for the water to boil, she joined Velma at the table and looked around the room. She had been in Velma's kitchen only once before, when Walter gave her a tour of the house after it was built. The kitchen was painted fashionably in yellow and green, with imitation slate tiles on the floor and brightly-patterned curtains framing the windows above the sink.

On the counter next to the sink was the angel food cake, the pan upended on a ginger ale bottle. The kettle whistled, and Livy poured the tea.

"I'm expecting a baby," Velma said.

"Oh," Livy said. She thought a moment and stirred sugar into her tea. "Congratulations."

"Thank you," Velma said. "Walter will be pleased."

"Aren't you?" Livy said.

"Of course," Velma said, lifting her cup to her lips.

They sat at the kitchen table and sipped their tea in silence while the rain sounded steadily against the windowpanes. When Walter arrived an hour or so later, Livy refused his offer of a ride home in his car, preferring the cold October rain to keeping a secret from her brother, even if it would only be for a little while.

Mamalogue

Oubria Tronshaw

I found a picture of myself, buried among dusty, long forgotten things. It was like unearthing an artifact from civilizations past, a crumbling relic to sift between my fingers. In the photo, I was smiling. My eyes were all lit up. Shadows had not yet crept around my corners. My hands rested on intact hips, a pelvis not yet spread apart, years away (though not as many as I thought) from pushing bloody, flailing limbs from its unsuspected depths. Me, before the grips and sighs of motherhood.

I'll just go ahead and say the thing I'm not supposed to say. Being a mom is hard as hell and I don't always like my kids. It's alright if you judge me cuz to be honest, sometimes I judge myself. But I also know I just spoke a truth out loud that lots of mothers are too ashamed to say. You're welcome.

Everyone knows not to shake a baby. You can tell without even touching a baby that it's something to be handled with care. Delicate. Tender-skinned and gentle-like.

But there is something about a screaming baby that can make you forget what you know. Shrill notes that erase your soft drive, program you with an alien hardness.

> Maybe if we could talk to each other about it,
> we wouldn't feel like exploding alla time.
> I'm talking to you, woman.

It starts softly. His fingers like fireflies light on my nipples. I flick them away, my hand the oblivious twitch of a horse's tail. His pelvis arches a question to my backside and I move away politely. Not a *no*, just a *not right now*. But it's a *not right now* too many. He gets out of the bed, pulling away the last mists of sleep with the sheet. Damn. Just because I don't want to fuck doesn't mean I don't want to cuddle.

Great Vagina Compromise of 6:59 am. I tell him, *I don't have any papers to grade this afternoon. The kids will be at daycare. We'll be alone.* He wants nothing of this treaty; he's been tricked before by the fine print. *Subject to approval. Certain conditions apply. Offer revoked in case of afternoon drowsiness, or a can't miss movie on TV, or a sudden case of the I-don't-feel-like-it-anymore's.* He tells me, *Nah, I won't be in the mood later.* And then the baby cries, and our sleepy-eyed son stumbles in asking for cereal. The alarm clock goes off again. We put down our word weapons. Flick the safety on our measured silences. Use our claws to carve a safe space in the tension for our children.

Sometimes I wonder if I would be better off as a single mother,

because then I could keep all my money.

I could raise my kids however I want.

I wouldn't have to open my legs and say, *quick,*

before the kids wake up,

when what I really want to say is

don't fucking touch me,

I need more sleep.

He tells me I should be his porn star. That we have to stay hot
for each other. What is hot? He wants to fuck me in the garage
on top of my mother's car, against the shed behind her house,
perched on top of her washer dryer. He wants me to strut for
him, prowl and mewl for him, let our babies cry and knock and
whine against the locked door while we pleasure each other. But
who can get pleasure from that? And who wants a woman who
could? How can he not understand that I'm somebody's mother
now?

Even though we were both naked, I'd made it clear that I didn't
want to make love. I told him I was too tired, which was code for
*you watch TV all day instead of looking for a job so we can move out of
my mother's house and this resentment I'm constantly swallowing
doesn't leave room in my mouth for me to do that thing you like.* Just
before I drifted off to sleep I heard him say, *I feel like you're going to
leave me.*

I've fallen down twice since finding out I'm pregnant again.
The first time, in the kitchen, I slipped on a slimy patch of dish liquid.
A month later I fell down the stairs in my stepmother's house. Both
times I waited for the tightening, the feel of a fist trying to break
through a plastic bag, and then blood on my (relieved?!?) panicked
thighs.

At my next doctor's appointment I harbored the secret hope
that there would be no heartbeat but there it was, strong as ever.
Piece by piece, the woman I had hoped to become is being carried away,
disposed of in diapers, washed down a river of runny noses,
kissed away by lips too busy talking to hear me: *I don't know if I can do
this.*

Maybe if we could talk to each other about it,
we wouldn't feel like exploding alla time.
I'm talking to you, woman.
Head in yo' hands, woman.
Breathless, wet eyed, busy fingered, woman.

I know what it be like, baby, believe me. I know what it's like cuz my
man ain't got no job either. And I feel bad at myself for feeling mad at
him alla the time. I know what it's like, get up early in the morning,
wanna sniff on yo' babies and cain't, have to walk away while they
crying. I been there. I know what it's like, looking back at their daddy
making breakfast, and you just wanna holler 'bout how wrong it feels to
leave them but you bend over instead, lace up your boots and save your
breath cuz the wind is picking up an' it's a long walk to the train
station.

I know what it be like to come home tired and aching, wanna put your
feet up and rest, but the house is a natural disaster. Crusty dishes,
snotty noses, sagging diapers, knotty heads, TV blasting, baby crying
for your tit before you can even get your coat off, kids hug your legs till
you damn near topple over, want to know *What's for dinner mama?* And
your man take a break from watching cable TV to come stick his tongue
down your throat and cup your booty cheek like how you used to like,
before your pussy dried up to make water for alla your tears.

My man, he look for work. He just don't find it. And I get so tired of
seeing his shoulders facing down that I tell him, *Don't worry baby, I can
swing things for awhile.* But then something heavy sits on my chest,
makes it hard to breathe. Somebody's grandmama shoulda wrote a
book or taught a class on how to deal with this. It's like a poison, the
resentment that seeps through my veins. I used to love when my
husband laughed but now I think, *What you got to smile about, broke ass?
We ain't got shit.* Sometimes he ask for money and I make him hand me
my purse. And then I ask for my change back, like he a child.

At night, sometimes I let him. Most times I say I'm too tired. When I do let him, I close my eyes and make my mind wander until it's done. I'm tired of him using me all up, not putting none back. Soon as he fall asleep the baby start crying, and this man snoring like he deaf. Wonder would he wake up if I slapped him cross his face? I feel tired in my bones, brittle like a paper doll.

Maybe if we could talk to each other about it,
we wouldn't feel like exploding alla time.
I'm talking to you, woman.
Head in yo' hands, woman.
Breathless, wet eyed, busy fingered, woman.
Tired of praying, *something's gotta give*, woman.
I'm talking to you.

No Woman's Land

Kara Provost

I don't want to drive the advertised mom-mobile
with the lay-down seats
so I can load up on antiques
I prowl the crowded aisles of flea markets for —
along with groceries, home improvements, my kids and two dogs
and of course cart the art I paint in my spare time,
no spare tire on me because I also run and do pilates.
(yoga is so yesterday, too sedate for a Botox mom).

I don't want to buy shin-guards and a team T-shirt,
enlist my daughter with the rest of the kindergarten girls
spend Saturdays at the field with other suburban parents,
rain or shine, while the kids run up and down
and we watch and cheer. Don't want to make
small talk at the bus stop, prick my writerly fingers
sewing costumes for the school play;
don't want to buy a cell phone for my sixth-grader to lose.
I don't want to go shopping
in the air-conditioned mall with her
to buy the latest, most expensive
distressed denim and pre-worn sweats;
don't want to wear Bermuda shorts and cut my long hair —
but I'm not wearing minis with stiletto heels
and I won't buy Blackest Midnight
to cover my silver streaks.

I'm neither here nor there, wandering around
in no-woman's land.
But come on out — the view is grand —
big expanse of sky and lots of fresh air.
I will not go gently
into that box-hedged, clip-lawned, pedicured
eternal empty day.

I Will Sleep No More Tonight
Carole Ann Moleti

The engine whines and glass breaks. Inanimate, hungry jaws crush and devour pieces of my life, and then the truck moves along to the next house and a new pile of junk. Impassionate and objective, it transforms once precious mementoes, stinking refuse, and junk into an anonymous mixture to be spit out in a dump or turned into glasphalt for paving the potholed streets. I will sleep no more tonight.

Eighteen years ago, after thirty-six hours of huffing, puffing and pushing, the squalling blue newborn, slick with blood and amniotic fluid, rested on my chest. Frightened eyes, fringed by impossibly long lashes, calmed as I crooned and stroked him. In that instant, I was transformed from a carefree woman into a mother and never slept soundly again.

For months, the toothless, wide-eyed infant nursed hungrily at my breast, flashing a sweet adoring smile and holding onto my finger for reassurance. My off-key songs were music to his delicate ears. Toddler cuddles and kisses bid me good morning and night, pushing me past the exhaustion into maternal nirvana.

On the first day of kindergarten I cried, even though he'd been in daycare since the age of six months, sensing that time would soon spiral away; the years ticked off by grades—first, second, third, fourth, fifth, middle and high school—interrupted by PTA meetings, bake sales, class plays, report cards, and math tutors.

At age nine, a boy with bright eyes, a pug nose and mushroom haircut, with cowlicks in the same places as me, played street hockey with his friends, furious because I insisted that he wear a helmet and wrist guards. Those implements of motherly torture, the hockey stick with the tattered orange Toys "R" Us price tag still attached and moldy rollerblades unearthed from a basement closet, have just been broken to bits, taken away by a vehicle designed to obliterate clutter, condemning attached emotions to death or partial resurrection by snapshots in a dusty album. I will sleep no more tonight.

That little boy is gone, too, replaced by a pony-tailed young man on Facebook smiling sweetly in a picture with his "friend that is a girl." He inherited my lack of singing talent but plays guitar like his idol Kirk Hammet of *Metallica*, swaying and head banging, long tresses flailing in defiance. The beard and moustache make him resemble Jesus Christ, though the language that spews from his mouth, and the skulls and chains adorning his black clothes, seem more inspired by Satan.

The bright light of enthusiasm and confidence I saw when he ran to play hockey with neighborhood friends flashed across his face when he left for college. I remain forever and unapologetically his mother, but he is no longer my baby.

I creep downstairs and stare out the window. The hockey stick, which had stuck up like a lighthouse over the choppy sea of years, has been snuffed out. Empty pails, tossed by a wintry gale, roll around the snowy street. Eighteen years of memories are carried away in the back of a lumbering vehicle, never to be seen again.

My husband, who insisted we get rid of all the junk, shuffles into the kitchen and surveys me in the dim light. "Are you all right?"

"My stomach is bothering me," I say, which is partially true. I don't mention the heartache.

Reassured, he goes back to bed. As a father, he is unable to understand why I will sleep no more tonight. In the dark and quiet he, the dog, cat, garden and other two children that occupy my life seem far away and unimportant. Tears run down my face. I scrawl and immortalize my memories before they scatter like dust in the wind and fade in the light of a new day.

Open House
Rita Moe

Nearly eighteen years ago today
in the middle of the night in a hospital room
this same boy was brought to you by a nurse.

Sitting up in bed. Transfer
of the blanketed bundle
from her arms to yours.

What you thought would be instinct
for both of you, needs to be taught
to both of you.

Your son's head must be turned
toward your body by the nurse.
Her fingers must coax his mouth open.

Unaccountably, someone else's breasts
are attached to your chest—
as swollen and hard as winter squash.

The blunt, hard end of one of these
is stuffed into your infants' mouth,
again and again

until, finally, he stays latched
and begins to suckle.
Then you are alone again and slip

into the nightmare you have had all your life —
you are drowning on your own tongue —
a nightmare you always struggled against

but now you stop flailing
and will yourself
to sink into it.

Your tongue swells,
fills all of you,
chokes and consumes you,

and you wake,
sweating, to realize this mystery
which has flooded over you

as far back as you can remember
must be a nursing memory from your own infancy,
a near suffocation from a time before words.

Now, eighteen years later, your son stands
in front of you. His name and *Congratulations!*
are written on a cake the size of his first crib.

According to the clock, in three minutes,
the entire graduating class of 300 and all of your relatives,
even those you'd prefer to forget, will be flooding into your home.

You are holding a bowl of potato salad
as if it is a life buoy when you hear him ask —
probably for the third time — where the camera is.

And you realize you have lost the words
for "desk" and "drawer."
You can only point at the wooden object

against the wall and make
in and out motions with one hand,
still cradling the bowl in your arms.

SELF-ACCEPTANCE

Aging's Arithmetic

Charlotte Mandel

Her years add by subtraction,
subtract by addition:

Wine-dark stains decorate skin,
upper arms do a shimmy dance.

Fingers that pry
frozen food packs in markets

bleach to color
of compacted desert,

skeletal tree root. It
catches her breath to see

how blood may exit
hands alive and in use.

Why I Changed My Name

mariana mcdonald

People change their names for lots of reasons.

For those brought across the Atlantic in dark horror and teeming illness, names were just one of many things robbed from them. New and unfathomable European names were slapped on them like the shackles they wore.

For immigrants, changing names was a matter of survival. Going from Kovalosky to Rand, or Steinberg to Stone, is a way for the new immigrant to escape the dangers of prejudice, to change his or her name to something deemed acceptable in the new world.

For those who have taken action to stand up to tyranny and are driven into a clandestine world, a new name is part of a new life as a political fugitive. In the face of repression, a trumpet player-turned-revolutionary named Filiberto becomes the gardener Don Luis.

Another name-change happens with those who have seen or experienced something that puts them in danger, and they undergo not only a name but an identity change in order to survive. This kind of name-change includes those persons—mostly women—who utilize an underground network to flee intimate partner violence and death threats against themselves and their children.

For transgendered persons, a name change is part of an overall process of change—social, emotional, physical, and spiritual—to a gender that matches who they are.

For those who seek fame and a new life in the lights, of Hollywood or New York or Paris, a new name is standard. Norma

Jean to Marilyn, Margarita Cansino to Rita Hayworth. Often these name changes are done to mask racial, ethnic, or religious identities that would narrow the would-be cultural commodity's range of commercial acceptance, like Richard Valenzuela becoming Ritchie Valens in the Mexican-unfriendly 1950s.

A pseudonym is common in writing; a *nom de plume* is taken up for a range of reasons. Perhaps the writer admires someone and decides to take their name, as Neftali Reyes Basoalto did in becoming Pablo Neruda. Or, in the hopes of enlarging the potential audience, a writer like Mary Anne Evans may deem she's better off as George Eliot, appearing as a man.

For women, there are two times when changing names is to be expected, though the first of these is slowly coming undone. It used to be (and in some cultures and classes still is) that a woman automatically changed her name when she got married—something that is also expected—from the name of her father to the name of her husband. One imposed name, if you will, to another.

This name change is documented, recorded, and considered thereafter the legal representation of the woman's name. The name she grew up with is then called her "maiden" name, her prior appellation retrospectively presented as a social chastity belt.

The second time many women change their name is when, quite differently, they change to something universal, timeless. It's when they become a mother (also expected), and in the moment of birth they go from Julia or Fatima or Elizabeth or Wangari to mother, mami, mama, mommy—all variations of the new identity summed up in a name that will never be documented as such, but will be the woman's name forever.

This kind of name-change—a change that embraces a new role or path in life—is one that has a rich history among people who have taken on new names voluntarily, intentionally, consciously.

Malcolm Little becomes Malcolm X. Agnes Bojaxhiu becomes Mother Teresa. Isabella Baumfree becomes Sojourner Truth.

This is the name-change tradition I embrace.

I didn't change my name when I got married. I wanted to keep the name that I had walked my thirty-some years with as a feminist and activist for women's rights. And I didn't want to hyphenate. The poet in me couldn't tolerate the pebble-mouthing result. When my father died, I became attached to my last name as a way of keeping him near me. I lived and wrote under the name I was given at birth.

But things changed. My husband, born in Puerto Rico, was diagnosed with a terminal illness when our children were young. That diagnosis began a long and painful road that turned many of our dreams to dust. When we had discussed getting married, we talked about moving to Puerto Rico. That was the plan: to leave the States and live there.

The last time he and I went to Puerto Rico together, I was carrying his ashes in a wooden box in my backpack, to scatter them in the Río Casei.

In the nine years of his illness, I took on a role that would become more important than caregiver. I realized that if my children were to grow up with a Puerto Rican identity they were proud of, if they were to know their history and culture, their great *herencia*, it would be my job to ensure it. I had long known Spanish, and had learned a good deal about Puerto Rican history in the course of my freelance journalism and activism. But that was not enough. My children needed to see their heritage, feel it, embrace it, and I had to create ways for that to happen.

My husband and I had always planned to raise the children to be bilingual, and we were aware of the standard guidance that one parent each consistently speak one language, as the way for it to be successful. But this was not something we could do; his ability to engage in this plan was rapidly diminished, and there were many days I felt I had words in *no* language.

But I could take our children to Puerto Rico, help them begin to know their father's country. So I did. We went in connection with a work conference and traveled the island for two weeks. We visited relatives and sites and got to visit the town my daughter is named for — the site of first insurrection against the Spanish in 1868 — and met the family of the patriot for whom my son is named. My hope for the trip was that they might begin to feel a connection with their heritage. My hopes were more than met: my children began to identify as Puerto Rican, began to seek out more of their history, began to proudly call themselves *Boricua*. As did I.

With each day that my husband got sicker, I became more and more Puerto Rican-identified. Relatives called me "honorary Puerto Rican" and I was mindful of what an honor it is. In my work, I began to be involved in Latino health, launching one of the first Latino health outreach projects in New Orleans. When we moved to Atlanta, I continued this focus.

I've written poetry in English most of my life. A few years ago I began writing poetry in my second language, a process that is nothing short of exhilarating.

My husband always called me Mariana. I loved hearing him say it, loved the sound of it. I loved, too, that it was the name of the woman who sewed the flag at Lares, Mariana Bracetti of the brave action that is known today as *El Grito de Lares*, the cry of Lares.

Over the years I had become more integrated into the Atlanta Latino community, and I always introduced myself as Mariana. But outside the Latino community I used my given name, which more and more rang less than true for me. In the spring of 2012, I decided to change my name in a way that would make it clear to many: I changed it on Facebook. Shortly thereafter, I decided to change my writing name as well.

At an artists' residency in the summer of 2012, I introduced myself to all those in the community (none of whom were Latino) as Mariana. Some had a hard time with it—both saying it right and the very idea of it. It puzzled some that I could have such a European, Irish-sounding last name and be a Mariana.

I write this essay to explain.

First and foremost, I changed my name to let my name speak for me. I want my name to tell people who I am, not who I'm not.

I changed my name to honor those who have called me Mariana all these years—beginning with my beloved husband.

I changed my name so I can float in the Caribbean.

I changed my name so I can walk in Neruda.

I changed my name to be one with Lares and all it signifies.

I changed my name to match my flag.

I changed my name to revel in the lilting sound of it, the ocean turning, mah-ree-ahh-nah. Said quickly, it's a bar of music: *Mariana*.

In sum: I simply could not keep it as it was!

Recently, in the course of my work, a colleague pulled me aside and asked, "So are you Puerto Rican?" I told her I am *boricua de corazón*—Puerto Rican by heart—and by history, not by birth. My life circumstances presented the responsibility to act in a way that gave my children access to their Puerto Rican heritage, and in the process I was transformed. It was both a duty and an opportunity, for which I am deeply grateful.

I was born with a different name in a different era, a name of another time and place. A place of highland flings and Bobbie Burns, tartans and bagpipes and kilts. All good and wonderful things. All part of a beautiful culture, but not so much mine now.

I am a bicultural person. I acknowledge the influences of my childhood and upbringing, but I get antsy when I don't speak Spanish for more than a few days, and for me the holidays are not regaled with a stuffed turkey but with *arroz con gandules*. I have fond memories of the dozens of different kinds of cookies my mother made for Christmas, filling the kitchen with an avalanche of decorated tins. But now the treat I relish making is flan, its golden juices the harbinger of special occasions.

Might I one day change my last name to the name of my children — and late husband? Perhaps.

But I am bicultural, and the name mariana mcdonald–my name–is just that.

And suits me fine.

Grasping the Een-gu-leesh
Jessica Caudill

My aunt Michelle watches a DVD she brought from China to help her learn English. The DVD goes through two hundred words, mostly basic ones. Rather, the words are basic to Americans. To a foreigner trying to learn each one, they might seem like a never-ending stream of jumbled letters; words that sound the same but are spelled differently, and who has time to learn the difference between "your" and "you're?" Some Americans can't even get it straight, and the sad part is they don't think it's a big deal as long as they've got something called "swag."

What is this "swag" you speak of? You ask. That's a good question, and you've asked the wrong person because I don't have a fucking clue. All I know is that this neologism is swiftly infecting the American lexicon, and it's almost as annoying as the acronym YOLO—that's "carpe diem" for cool kids. Shakespeare used the word "swaggering" in *A Midsummer Night's Dream*, but I am sure he wasn't using it in the same context as Lil' Wayne and Justin Bieber. And it's my hope, though I highly doubt it will happen, that Michelle doesn't try to integrate these and other slang terms that plague the English language like an etymological epidemic into her vocabulary. She has a difficult enough time learning the variations and pronunciations of English words—and even *how* to say them when conveying certain meanings, words that are likely not contained on the disk she pops into the DVD player and watches, wide-eyed, and repeats back to the tooth-bearing instructor on the screen.

"This is my A-B-C DVD!" she told me one day as she held up the disk so I could see the label. It was colorful and cute, with bubbly letters and smiling faces of kids.

My uncle Mardell laughed. "Michelle, that DVD is for children!"

Michelle lowered the disk in her hand and stomped to the media room.

"Ugh, *for children!*"

The DVD is good for auditory stimulation, but Michelle can get that from everyday conversation.

What she does the most is copy choice phrases from a lesson manual into her spiral notebook. She writes down everything verbatim from the manual, and for some of the translated words or phrases she uses red ink; things she says often or has the most trouble remembering. The covers are creased, and the pages are soft with turned corners. Mardell asked her, "Why are you doing that, Michelle?" Everything is already printed in the manual, why take the time to copy it from one book to another? I think it's a matter of kneading the words into the doughy gray matter. There's an article floating around the web called "The Positive Effects of Writing Practice on Integration of Foreign Words in Memory," which says that, based on experimental findings, the brain encodes and stores unfamiliar words better when they are copied by hand. This takes me back to my elementary school days when the teacher assigned a new list of words each week for spelling tests. Every week, we students had to write each word on the list five times as practice. As you write down a word, you might say each letter aloud or to yourself. You're actively focusing on the task at hand (pardon the pun).

In her book *Write It Down, Make It Happen*, author Henriette Anne Klauser says that "Writing triggers the RAS, which in turn sends a signal to the cerebral cortex: 'Wake up! Pay attention! Don't miss this detail!'" Located at the base of the brain, the reticular activating system, or RAS, is like a mega-filter that sorts out every piece of information that enters your brain. It categorizes the information and gives priority to what you're concentrating on at any given moment, allowing for better attention and recall.

What can we learn from all of this? The one thing we were taught that makes perfect: *practice, practice, practice* so the words will be stored in long-term memory. These things can certainly be of help when a person is trying to learn a second language. However, the pen is not a magic wand that waves around as you're writing down foreign words and then suddenly you're able to speak back what you've just written down with perfect diction. Somewhere during the language-learning process, Broca's area must step in to assist the tongue and mouth to move properly as each word is spoken. Otherwise, words get mispronounced, something that can leave a bad taste in one's mouth. Take the word "horror," for example. It's a word that Michelle struggles with. As she was busy writing down phrases and conversation starters in her notebook, such as "How did you like the scary movie?" and saying the words aloud, Mardell was helping her with pronunciation. The conversation shifted to Michelle's distaste for horror movies.

"*Horror movie* and *scary movie* mean the same thing," Mardell said.

Michelle wrote the variations down in her notebook and spoke them aloud. She sounded like a little girl writing a letter to Santa: Dear...Santa...I...have...been...a good...girl...this... year. But Michelle's Broca's area hasn't yet tuned itself to many English words. So when she said the word "horror" she left out that last soft syllable. She sounded more like she was asking a friend if he had enjoyed watching a, shall we say, risqué film.

"How...did...you...like...the...*hor*...movie?"

Cue Professor Higgins to the rescue. "No no no. Those words don't mean the same thing, Michelle. It's horror, *horr-or*. Don't say 'whore' A whore is a woman who likes to sleep with too many men."

Michelle said, "Ah! Maybe I will just say 'scary movie.' I don't like too many men. Maybe in another life I like too many men."

"In China," Michelle told me, "my language was not the same as other Chinese people." This confused my American brain at first. I know there are different dialects spoken in China, but completely separate languages?

"I speak the Hong Kong language," she continued. In her book, *Dreaming in Chinese: Mandarin Lessons in Life, Love, and Language*, Deborah Fallows explains that, because of the diverse dialects in China, sometimes Chinese people have trouble communicating with each other: "Although speakers of the Sichuan dialect and of standard Mandarin can understand each other pretty well, they wrestle over the tones, which are different."

Tone is something Michelle struggles with, even if she knows a word or phrase very well. Sometimes when she speaks she sounds robotic, like Microsoft Sam, *"What-would you-like for-lunch?"* Could the problem be her loose grasp on the use of English tones, the way she was taught English, or both? Fallows writes that one Chinese woman she talked to was taught English in "a very rote way…with each new word pronounced with a falling tone." When asking someone a question, the woman had to make a conscious effort to add a rising tone to the word at the end of the sentence. The issue wasn't that she didn't know what to say, but rather she didn't know *how* to say it. When Michelle reads from her notes, she can't hear the tones in her head. The A-B-C DVD instructors might sound like they're chanting where every word has a low, monotonous falling tone, "Hàt, bàll, gò, stòp…"

Likewise, I have trouble deciphering tones in Michelle's language. It's sometimes amusing to listen to the conversations she has with her friends and family on her webcam. At times I think they're fighting the way they talk to one another, rapidly and sometimes loud as if engaging in a passionate debate. There are almost no lapses in conversation, no pauses except when the other person is talking. They give one another half a second to breathe before picking up again. They seem to never run out of things to talk about. Sometimes they sound like they're singing to each other when tone and pitch rises and falls.

Although Mandarin has a fraction of the number of syllables as English, the language is, according to Fallows, "flooded with homonyms." Speakers of Mandarin make up for their inventory of 400 syllables by applying about four tones to each syllable, making for a seemingly unlimited combination of words and meanings. Some Asian languages have more tones than that: Cantonese has seven, for example. How many different ways do you think you could pronounce the word "bark" and have it mean more than "the sound a dog makes" or "the skin of a tree?"

Westerners are taught, though not so much anymore, it seems, to say "please" and "thank you" in an array of social situations. Those words are meant to show respect and appreciation. "Thank you" I hear Michelle say from time to time, and she says it in a borderline whisper, as if she'd rather not say it. But I don't recall ever hearing her say "please." Fallows says, "The Chinese way of being polite to each other with words is to shorten the social distance between you. And saying please serves to insert a kind of buffer or space that says, in effect, that we need some formality between us here." A Chinese woman says to her brother at the dinner table, "Give me the salt," or simply, "Salt!" Not a "please" or "thank you" is uttered to the brother. Rude? Not in this case. The

Chinese view friends and family as extensions of themselves. Why ask yourself to *please* pass the salt, and then thank yourself for the action? My take on all of this is that, to the Chinese, saying "Please pass the salt" to your brother may mean another word that begins with the letter "r": redundant. The Chinese see these words inserted into requests or questions as excessive, maybe even condescending. Consider the following inner dialogue of any given individual at dinner time:

SELF: *Ahem.* Could you *please* pass the salt?

SELF: Excuse you? Get your own damn salt.

When Michelle trips up on a word or phrase, she repeats it over and over aloud, closing her eyes as if she's imagining the letters in her mind and her tongue is chasing after them. She sits at the kitchen table for hours at a time, mind surely traveling at the speed of light, head bent over her notebooks, eyes closed, leaned back in her chair, staring at the ceiling, mouth mimicking the words, hand dancing across the paper, copying letters in red ink, crossing letters out, *"Ai ya!"* reading back phrases over and over and over correcting herself, "Aren't you forgetting *shomesting-*

"sss*ome*-sting-

"some-*thiiiiing…*"

Whisper the word through clenched teeth, slowing down so she doesn't trip, with a single fist and extended index finger pointing at the notebook she tries one more time, *"Aren't…you…for-get-ting…"*

See the word, it's right there *point point point*

"…I forget."

A page full of scribbles and a day lost because of one word, "I forget, so tired, my eyes," she takes off her glasses and rubs them, "Oh, wrinkles. Wash face!"

Some days I think about calling to check on Michelle. The number is pulled up on my cell phone, a finger hovering over the "call" button, but I erase the number and put my phone back in my pocket. I can't tell you how many times I've done this. That's not important; the elephant in the room is the bigger question of "Why?" Why the hesitation, the fear that words will get lost in translation and erupt into an argument, a severing of family ties, and, heaven forbid, one less Christmas card to send every year?

The question *is* the answer. We are from opposite sides of the world and speak two different languages, both complicated and confusing in their own ways. Even the inflections are different, depending on the feelings you want to convey. Spoken in a loud, high-pitched voice, Michelle could very well be expressing through Chinese that she loves my new shoes, while I curl into the fetal position, thinking that she's telling me I look like a hooker. If you were, as the saying goes, to dig a hole to China, an introverted American girl like me would fall through a topsy-turvy rabbit hole and end up on a land where every day is Opposite Day. I know Michelle is busy trying to learn a new language, but someday I would like her to teach me a little Chinese. Maybe then I'd be more inclined to pick up the phone, punch in the numbers, and wait for her voice on the other side. My gut tells me that Michelle is waiting too.

Hair Story
Stephanie Gates

Now

Standing in the food court mall, I hear a woman talking on her phone. Because cell phones are the white noise of the new millennium, she quickly fades into the background as I concentrate on something *really* important—what to eat. Then I hear her say, "Excuse me. You are beautiful! That looks good on you. I just wanted to tell you that," she says with a nod and a smile. I thank her and feel myself grow as her comment reaches inside and soothes my soul. Here is a Black woman complimenting another Black woman on the way she wears her hair—short *and* natural. I am full, and I haven't eaten.

I love my hair! (or lack of it) and I believe people respond to my closely cropped natural hair because of the energy I send to the universe. Even though my hair has been the same length for more than a decade, and many people have only known me with it short, it is still a topic of conversation no matter where I go. In the airport a man asks, "Can I rub your head?" He is bald and says that women always ask to rub his head, so he wants to know what it feels like to rub someone else's. I laugh and oblige him even though I don't normally like people to touch my hair—one of my idiosyncrasies.

In this long-hair obsessed culture, it amazes people that I *choose* to wear mine short. It is especially an oddity in the African-American community, where women are forever chasing the elusive White

Girl Toss-and-Swing. Some say it takes confidence to do what I've done, and maybe it does. I've found what works for me, and I'm happy.

Then

I remember as a child in my community, those Blacks with European features and physical characteristics were favored. So, like many little girls of color, I wanted to be light, bright, and damned-near white with long, "good" hair and "pretty" eyes. My complexion is caramel, my eyes are light brown, and my hair at the time was shoulder length, so the only thing "wrong" with me was my hair texture. It needed to be grade A or better, but without Indian or mixed-raced blood in my family, the best I could hope for was B, with a little help from a hot comb. I couldn't have "good" hair in real life, so I made up for it in my fantasy life. All the women in my drawings at school had hair cascading down their backs.

When the Black is Beautiful wave hit, I was swept up in the pride of the moment. It was one of the happiest periods in my life. I was beautiful just the way I was because my seven-year-old self got a full taste of blackness. At the height of the Black Power movement, Black folks were sporting dashikis and afros, and the sound of James Brown's "Say It Loud—I'm Black and I'm Proud" reverberated in the air. The annual Easter ritual of the wash, press, and curl was replaced with the afro, and I wanted to convert. My forever-press-and-curl mother relented and let me wear a 'fro. There I was on Easter Sunday in a white dress with navy blue trim on the sleeves, a thin patent leather matching belt, and black patented leather shoes, all set off by an afro that was bigger than me.

What a beautiful, confident girl!

At school I began drawing men and women with huge afros and platform shoes. I accessorized the women with big hoop earrings and the men with sideburns. My teacher prohibited me from drawing people with afros, but after a conference with my sister, my teacher said I could draw people with afros as long as I made their naturals smaller. It didn't matter much because my afro fascination was short-lived, and I soon returned to the "real" world of long, straight hair, but the little girl with the big afro lived in my heart.

Now

I am sitting in the airport in Denver, dipping my overcooked chicken strips in some honey mustard sauce. *I really don't like airport food*, I am thinking to myself. An older white woman with a bleached blonde flip and false eyelashes sits on the stool at the counter next to me. She begins slicing and eating the polish sausage, but leaving the bread. *That's smart, a good way to cut down on carb consumption*, I mentally note to myself. She turns and tells me, "That haircut looks good on you."

"Thank you," I reply.
"It's a good cut for the summer."
I nod my agreement and continue eating.
I am full.

Tall
Brandy French

For as long as she could remember, Tookie Basch wanted to be tall, like one of those willowy teenagers with legs and necks like giraffes in *Vogue* and *Mademoiselle*. And one Monday morning in April, after a long night of vodka martinis and shameless flirtation with the keyboard player in the band at her married sister's 40th birthday party, Tookie woke up seven feet tall.

She was, admittedly, very hung over, but that could not account for why the blond oak floor was two extra feet from her eyes when she looked down. Or that her feet would no longer fit into her Fuzzy Froggy bedroom slippers.

She walked barefoot to the full-length mirror across from the bed, but she could only see herself from the waist down. She had to move backward, banging her head as she passed through the doorway into the hall, to get the whole picture. When she did, she cried out in shock.

"Oh, my God!"

Her husband, Dan, woke up long enough to shout, "What?" but when he saw through half-shut, myopic eyes that she was neither hanging from the ceiling fan nor lying naked and bloody from knife wounds, he promptly fell back to sleep.

This reassured Tookie, until she remembered that her husband had stopped noticing anything about her a couple of years earlier.

Born Karen Basch thirty-six years earlier, her mother called her Cookie, which her four-year-old sister Monica pronounced "Tookie," and Tookie stuck. Monica was tall like her mother and father, five foot eight by the time she reached fourteen, but Tookie was a runt, stopping her climb toward stature at a diminutive five foot three.

Tookie sat back down on her side of the bed and began to cry, her enlarged hands laying palms up in her lap like grapefruit halves.

"Oh my, oh my," she said.

Dan mumbled something about coffee and then reached over to the night table, first for his glasses and then for the clock to see if he could steal a few more minutes of sleep. He didn't have to be at Deloitte & Touche, where he was a senior accountant, until 9:20.

"Dan? Danny? Could you turn over and take a look at me?"

Her husband rolled over without curiosity and faced his wife's hunched-over back.

"What?"

She stood up and turned around to face him, her pale green nightgown barely reaching her meatless thighs. Her arms had lengthened toward her knees, which now looked knobby, and her legs, once thick with muscle from thousands of miles on the treadmill, had stretched into slender ropes.

"Holy shit."

They sat in Dr. Blechner's waiting room without an appointment because this was an emergency, Dan insisted, and they damn well needed some answers.

Dr. Blechner didn't have any.

"Good heavens," he said when he saw this woman he'd known for more than a decade. Tookie was wearing a pair of her husband's trousers that looked like shorts on her and a red plaid flannel shirt with unbuttoned sleeves that barely skimmed her elbows. The doctor checked Tookie's heart and lungs, took a urine sample, and then drew blood, shaking his head several times in the process as if shaking would jostle the situation into perspective.

"Have you ever seen anything like this before, Doctor?" Dan asked.

"Well . . ." Dr. Blechner said, pulling on one of his earlobes, "I've seen pictures of acromegaly in the textbooks. But I don't think this is acromegaly."

"Am I going to die?" Tookie asked, trying not to cry. She felt sure her condition was fatal.

"No, no," Dr. Blechner said reassuringly, but in truth he didn't have the slightest idea.

For the first time since their marriage six years earlier, Dan went clothes shopping with his wife.

"You can't go around wearing my clothes," he said. "They look ridiculous, and they don't even fit."

"I'm sorry," Tookie said as if she'd backed the car into their garbage cans or shrunk his favorite sweater.

He should have said it wasn't her fault but he wasn't convinced that was true. *She must have done something wrong,* he thought, but he just couldn't imagine what.

After Dan dropped Tookie off at home, hurrying downtown to his office in the Chicago Loop, she wandered around their Sheridan Road condo like a stranger. She discovered that the top of the refrigerator was black with greasy dirt and the corners of the kitchen had a network of dense aerial cobwebs.

When she searched the cabinet above the counter for peanut butter, she noticed that all her canned and packaged goods were crammed onto the two lowest shelves. Now, face to face for the first time with the empty third and fourth shelves, she realized that her height gave her new options. She shifted the flour, barley, sugar, and rice, the brownie mix, the macaroni and cheese, and the extra bottles of ketchup and soy sauce up to the top shelf, and the cans of salmon, sardines, tuna, and soup onto shelf three, leaving plenty of space for the peanut butter, pasta, simmer sauces, coffee, noodles, and the box of Splenda on the first and second shelves. Stepping back to admire her achievement, she felt exhilarated. Dare she even say empowered?

After making short work of the refrigerator top and the cobwebs, Tookie sat down in the breakfast nook with her coffee and peanut-buttered bagel and stared at her iPhone in the charger. She felt that she should call somebody, but she could not think of what to say. *Oh, hi, mom, guess what? I just grew two feet last night while I was sleeping.* She knew better than to give an hysteric like her mother a reason to become hysterical, and this was a really good reason. Of course, she would eventually have to tell her family. But now that Monica's 40th birthday had been put to rest, she didn't expect to see them for a while, which was fine with her.

Tookie decided to call her friend Wanda. Bizarre as it sounds, Wanda had been abducted by aliens from the Leda 25177 galaxy in the Hydra Supercluster when she was a pimply-faced teenager. They returned her to earth with clear skin and the formula for a spongy white mud that cured acne, which her parents subsequently sold to Merle Norman for a very large undisclosed amount. Tookie felt sure that Wanda, who thanks to the abduction was now independently wealthy, would know how to put Tookie's transformation in perspective.

"When I woke up this morning, I was seven feet tall," Tookie said when Wanda answered.

"Are you at work?"

"No. I called in sick." Tookie usually called Wanda from her office where she was an advertising media buyer.

"Are you sick?"

"No, but I'm seven feet tall, Wanda. Actually six foot eleven and a fourth. The doctor measured me."

"You went to see the doctor?"

"Dan thought a doctor would know what was going on."

"Did he know?"

"No, he wasn't sure."

"It's God's mysterious will," Wanda said, which was what she always said when strange things happened.

"Dan had to buy me a bunch of new clothes. He went with me to Marshall Field's."

"Well, that's good," Wanda said. "They have a lot of nice things there."

For the rest of the day, Tookie explored the upper half of the condominium. She replaced the burned out bulbs in the dining room chandelier, the track lights in the living room, and the carriage lamp in the entryway. She dusted the tops of the bookcases, which had not been touched since she and Dan moved in. She pruned and watered the hanging plants on the balcony, and she tackled the floor-to-ceiling windows with vinegar and newspaper.

Then she went outside and took a walk. She touched the soft, moist leaf buds that were opening on the oak tree branches, peeked into a robin's nest and counted three spotted blue eggs, and observed that most of the neighboring rain gutters were clogged with winter debris. She also discovered that she scared small dogs and startled old women, most of whom could only make eye contact with her navel. And every so often, if she stood on her toes, she caught a glimpse of the silver gray waters of Lake Michigan. Tookie began to think that short people were as tragically handicapped as the deaf and blind, and she imagined organizing a fundraiser to promote compassion and understanding for the vertically challenged. Waking up tall, she thought, was certainly not the worst thing that could happen to a person.

That night, Tookie put on the new black extra-long Marshall Field's nightie that Dan had bought her and for the first time tried to initiate their lovemaking.

"I'm a different woman now, Danny. Don't you think we should re-consummate our marriage?"

"I don't know," Dan said, shying away from her. At five foot nine, he barely came to the top of her chest. "You feel like a stranger to me, Took, I can't help it."

"I thought men liked new women," she said.

"Not this new," Dan said.

"Well, it's not new down there," she said, pointing to her crotch.

"How do you know?" he said. "Everything else is different."

"Not my breasts," she said.

"That's true," Dan agreed sadly. "They're as small as ever."

"You're such a shit," Tookie said, surprising herself with the exclamation, and she wanted to say even more. But instead she just crawled into the bed, which was now a foot too short for her legs, and wept.

55

Tookie woke up very early the next morning and got into the office at 7:30. After Dan's reaction the night before, she was determined to avoid attention. But when *The Morning Show* caterer went past her office in the hallway at 9:30, Tookie called to her, hoping that if she stayed seated, the girl wouldn't notice her height. Tookie craved something sweet like a cinnamon bun or a maple bar, and now that she was almost as tall as a bean stalk, she could eat anything she wanted without worrying about getting fat. It would have been great if only she weren't so freakishly tall! Six feet would have been plenty, she thought, but her situation was like Alice and the eat-me pills.

Almost the same thing had happened to Tookie when she was twelve and wished for breasts. She went from nothing to a C-cup practically overnight and got teased for being "chesty." Then she lost *too* much of it when she was on Weight Watchers in her twenties and never got it back. You had to be careful what you wished for, she thought, making a mental note.

Fortunately, the lunch date she'd scheduled was with a new client, NaturalCat Organic Cat Food, so he wouldn't look shocked when she met him at the restaurant. She spent all morning tweaking her media plan, carefully addressing the changes her boss Luther had requested to beef up the organic-only pubs. She stopped only long enough to respond to Wanda's text message urging her to contact Oprah or Dr. Oz.

At noon, Tookie left the agency by a side door, feeling relieved that she'd survived the morning without being outed.

❖

Evan Collier was waiting for her at the bar when she arrived at The Gage, one of the trendy new downtown lunch venues. She was relieved to see that his cocktail was a Perrier with lime, because her last Cat client had been a raging alcoholic. Better still, Collier was tall, over six feet two, she estimated, although he only came up to her chin.

"Delighted to meet you," he said, grasping her hand and looking her over with what seemed like genuine interest. He had the kind of man's face that usually came with a dusty Stetson and a big open sky. Tookie had been stooping a little when she approached him, but his smile made her stand up straight.

How she ended up at the Hotel Sofitel Water Tower that afternoon, wrapped in Evan Collier's burly arms, she could not explain— although the two apple martinis she downed probably smoothed the way. She had not only betrayed her husband, she had violated a cardinal rule of business. Of course, she knew that plenty of people, including her boss Luther, violated that rule, but it was so unlike Tookie. What was it about being tall that had changed her so profoundly? And the worst of it was that she wasn't even sorry. She hadn't let herself realize until today how neglected she'd felt, how unnoticed, how unappreciated by Dan. This man, Evan Collier, had made love to her like she was a gorgeous sensual gazelle, delighting in her long limbs and soft skin and sweet taste. No, she definitely was not sorry. And if he asked her to join him for another romantic rendezvous, or even a runaway weekend in Belize, she just might say yes, and yes, and yes.

When Tookie returned to her office at Leo Burnett late that afternoon, she no longer tried to hide. She strode through the lobby with a big smile on her face and laughed with enjoyment when the receptionist gaped at her. *Get used to it, people,* she thought.

"What the hell *happened* to you?" her boss Luther said when she came into his office. "You look like a goddam flamingo!"

"I had a growth spurt," she said, and sat down in his love seat, crossing her legs in the becoming manner that only tall women execute properly. "By the way, the lunch went well. Evan signed off on the plan without any changes."

"Really? I heard he was a sonovabitch," Luther said, holding his stubbly jowls in the cup of his hand.

"Not to me," Tookie said, smiling provocatively. She knew Luther wouldn't believe what she'd been up to that afternoon even if she showed him a videotape, but it was fun to tease him a little.

"What the hell happened to *you*?" he said again with a low, soft whistle.

That night, after Tookie slid under the covers with her husband, she said, "We'll have to get a bigger bed."

"Maybe you'll wake up tomorrow and be short again," Dan said, continuing to read the latest Alex Cross mystery. He seemed to have lost interest in his wife's predicament once Dr. Blechner couldn't diagnose it.

"I wouldn't count on it," Tookie said, although the thought made her a little anxious.

"Well, we'll just have to make the best of it," he said, which was Dan's way of telling her he had stopped listening.

Later that night, Tookie's cold toes woke her up and she went into the kitchen to make herself a cup of herbal tea. She augmented it with a leftover slice of red velvet birthday cake from her sister Monica's party, scraping the remnants of cream cheese frosting off the plate with her fork.

In the soft light of the kitchen dimmers, she examined her legs and arms, stretching them out to their full lengths and taking deep, relaxing breaths. *Goddam flamingo!* she thought, smiling at the recollection. She realized that this bizarre transformation had given her more than height. It had given her perspective, enabled her to — what was that expression? — to see the forest for the trees. The stove clock said 2:10, but she did not feel pressured to return to bed. She savored all the tiny sounds that punctuated the night's silence, the refrigerator motor, the ice maker, a window's hoarse rattle as a car sped past outside, even the soft click of the clock hand to 2:11.

Tookie wondered what she'd look like when she woke up in the morning. Short again? Taller — god, she hoped not taller. Blond? Blond would be okay. Poor Dan, then he'd really be confused. His wife, a tall, a *very* tall, willowy blond. But why not? Maybe she'd do that anyway. Evan Collier would probably love it.

Tookie decided that her friend Wanda was right. Whatever happened, it was God's mysterious will. *Somebody's* mysterious will, at any rate, she thought, and while it meant that some poor soul in Prague might wake up one morning as a cockroach, on a different morning a hundred years later, a woman in Chicago could just as well wake up tall.

Lawn Shots
Jen Cullerton Johnson

The sun hangs low behind the branches of the willow tree.

My white blouse buttons down the front; the neck clasp missing opens to a patch of pale, freckled skin. Dirt rings around my Peter Pan collar from a week's worth of wear. A heart-shaped gold locket dangles between my undershirt. The name engraved on the locket belongs to my mother. The letters in tight cursive spell out *Patricia*, her name my lips repeat, like a prayer. If I say *Patricia* enough, she won't disappear but stay like her locket around my neck.

Faded navy knee socks, mismatched and slack, fall into my gym shoes from last year. My scotch plaid skirt of blue and green with a hint of yellow hangs to my knees, like a wet towel. Bangs cut straight across cover my worried forehead and drop into the lashes of my brown eyes, eyes the color of tree bark, the same bark of the willow tree my back leans up against. My lilac school bag, empty except for two pencils and a notebook, lounges at my feet.

My father's drink of one-one-thousand, two-one-thousand, three-one-thousand count-outs of scotch slosh in his Waterford glass. His Brooks Brothers suit wrinkles at his knee and elbow. Hours ago, my last day of third grade ended, but now, like a camera-toting Lazarus, my father resurrects this day to document his daughter's last day of school.

The sun slips lower. The streetlights glow.

"Smile, like you mean it this time," my father says.

Tripod legs extend in front of him. Lenses and camera bag litter our overgrown lawn. A trick of light, a shadow, a shade, my father newly widowed, seeks to bring back what his camera can never render: a family whole and full, a life with his wife by his side, a happy daughter like in those old and fingerprinted negatives in the basement.

No smile comes.

My father's voice slurs from the amber liquid. "Why can't you just smile a little?"

My eyes cast down in the dust around the roots of the willow tree. My gym shoes slash at roots. The corners of my mouth ache. No smile comes. The tripod tips. His camera sways. He snaps another then another. The streetlights glare in the evening night.

"One more time," my father says, swallowing the last remains in his glass. "Do it for me, huh? *Smile.*"

I just stood there.

TSEBROCHENER:
A Story for the Broken
Jessica Glover

Something inside me had broken,
though I tried to hold it in. Red, on everything.
--"Flowers" by Kathleen Fraser

Standing naked in my bathroom, staring into the mouth of the toilet bowl, the water was actually beautiful, swirling from pink to carmine. I stood, staring, until my legs started to quiver and the red rivulets running down them turned brown and hardened. I stared until I began to construct some face in the fetal tissue staring back at me like a macabre Rorschach test. No head. No fingers. It was barely even a blob, but there was mass to it. When it slipped from inside me, the mass was large enough to make a sound hitting the water. Then, it lay on the bottom of the bowl, halfway down the drain already. I stared, thinking it should float on the water. It should float.

At some point my knees gave and I fell onto the linoleum. The skin over my left kneecap busted open and a fresh stream of blood seeped slowly around the white base of the toilet. I didn't feel any pain; I felt absolutely nothing. I could not bring myself to move, so I stayed sprawled diagonally across the tiny bathroom. My cat, the only witness, cried and crawled over my hipbone into the puddle. He cried louder, sniffed, and began to knead red paw prints on my stomach and chest. I tried to think about what a normal woman would do after her first miscarriage. Do normal women have miscarriages? What kind of woman am I?

What came next was not a dream because I wasn't asleep. I was awake, but I could not move. I knew what I needed to do. I needed to stop my knee from bleeding. I needed to clean my cat's paws. I needed to flush the toilet . . . but I couldn't. I knew it had to be done. I couldn't leave it sitting halfway down the drain forever. I couldn't call someone to pull the lever for me. For a moment, I thought how embarrassing it would be if a neighbor or friend stopped by to find me in such a state.

I was the only one who could fix the mess. The responsibility, the finality, immobilized me. I couldn't even raise my head from the floor. Ephemerally, thoughts surfaced and then regressed out of my grasp, so I tried to hold one image in my mind. I tilted my head toward the bathroom's door frame and stared down the hall at a patch of carpet where *he* had stood dripping wet before he grabbed my guest towel, dried, dressed, and left me weeks before. I wanted him to walk over, lift me up, and carry me back to his loft where I could dream this away and wake up to chocolate chip pancakes and kisses down the small of my back.

Instead, his image walked into the bathroom and squatted down before me. I knew he wasn't really with me, he was thirteen weeks in at Texas Tech by then, but I couldn't face reality. I let the image enter. He placed his face on the linoleum in front of mine, but even his face was too complex to focus on. At first, he seemed to be completely expressionless, showing no sign of understanding or forgiveness. Why should he care? He had made his choice to leave months ago. Why should he offer any form of assistance now? Still, I longed for any hint that suggested he sympathized. His features quickly began to blur until just a smile remained. I focused on his upturned lips for three hours.

All girls grow up with an acute awareness of the simple pain that accompanies childbirth. We know of the ripening and splitting that our body will one day endure. We carry dolls that piss and burp and repeat "I love you, Mommy" until we are old enough to prefer the perfectly molded plastic Barbie. In a way, I would have been prepared for pregnancy. This was something wholly opposite. This was complicated and effortless at the same time. I didn't even have to strain for that slightest weight to slip from me. I felt immensely close to death. The sound of it, of the mass dropping into the water, slowly circled over me like dusty blades on a ceiling fan slicing around in my subconscious. I could hear it constantly reminding me; it rubbed my mind sore. The desire to stop the spinning engulfed me, and, without raising my head, I tried to drown out everything by flushing the toilet. Then, I was left sinking in the rummy silence of the room.

In order to have faith it is important to believe that everything in the world carries meaning. In that moment, I searched for meaning imperatively. A lesson from my father floated from the burnished pulpit of my childhood, returned to me: The Yiddish word *tsebrochen* means not simply "heartbroken" but "completely broken," with the implication that parts are not just broken but missing as well. A *tsebrochener* is a person who is broken and far from whole.

I was not heartbroken . . . I was completely broken. Broken and alone. The cat had long abandoned me, and I could follow his red-splotched prints down the hall. The only person who might have grieved the loss had left after drunken sex and a promise to keep in touch. That was three months before, and I had not received one word from Mr. I'll-Call-When-I-Get-to-Lubbock.

Slowly, details began to sharpen until everything seemed absolutely lucid. I became aware of the heat blowing from the vent above me, the mildew in the cracks of the tub's tile, and, eventually, the honeyed blood fixing me to the floor. I climbed into the bathtub with a desperate need to destroy all evidence. I emptied an entire bottle of cheap soap and scrubbed the body that betrayed me. My skin turned blotchy; the washcloth turned pink. I continued to scour the walls, the corners, the faucet, and the showerhead. I followed the paw prints over the ledge of the tub onto the floor. I climbed out of the bath, grabbed my toothbrush from the sink, and continued with the grout of each tiled square. I dumped handfuls of water over the toilet and sopped the linoleum. I drained the tub and then rinsed it over and over and over. I avoided the mirror. I snatched up piles of towels and covered the entire room. Furiously, I rubbed every inch dry until only pure white remained. I rubbed and polished until I could imagine my mother coming over and exclaiming, "You always were such a tidy child, just look how spotless this bathroom is." Afterwards, I climbed back into the tub, pulled the faucet to a hard left, and let the water scald.

Life turned real perfect afterward.

That's the lie I kept trying to make myself believe in the following weeks. I had been coping by ignoring everything. Three days after the miscarriage, I passed out walking to art class. I started skipping gym appointments not only because I was too tired to work out but because I overslept for them entirely. I laid in the tanning booth long after the lights went off trying to stay warm. I threw up anything that touched my lips, and I continued to convince myself that nothing was wrong.

It was a Sunday night, and I was waiting tables. I ignored the first few drops of blood I noticed while in the ladies room. The lighting was dim in the stall, and my tables were growing impatient for fresh loaves of bread. The sharp pain ratcheting across my waist started a few minutes after I delivered the bread. By the time I was standing over the toilet again, blood was soaking through and I was thankful the uniform required black pants and apron. Blood on black, who would notice?

In the dining room, Italian lovers warbled from the stereo system. Sunday drivers casually strolled in for a nibble. The kitchen inevitably backed up. I pushed a cart of glass racks stacked six deep from the dish pit to the bartender. The same hazy feeling flooded over me, only this time I wasn't shielded in my apartment. Halfway to the bar my body began to cry out strenuously against me. I clutched the cart and doubled over. I scanned the faces in the room, a few already glancing at me, but *he* was not there. The sound of thirty-two wine glasses crashing to the cement floor was the last thing I heard. I imagined the sensation resonated from inside of me, a steep crescendo until I was completely shattered, completely broken.

I remember throwing my full bed pan at the night nurse like some crazed monkey girl who ripped out her IV and yelled *ten, ten, ten* when asked about the pain level. The first five days in the hospital had been a blur, but nothing bothered me. On the sixth night they stopped my morphine drip, and I was awake with pain. The three attempts to insert a catheter had been unsuccessful due to extreme dehydration, even the retired Army nurse didn't have any luck. This wasn't an issue since my lower intestines had shut down, but after the surgery three bags of fluid had been pumped through me. I needed help simply walking across the room to the toilet that didn't flush.

The night nurse left me screaming into the little speaker strapped to the bed rail *ten, ten, ten.* Her voice would static back, calmly saying she had given me the maximum dose of morphine signed off by the doctor. She infuriated me. The room, the sterile whiteness, and my family whispering in the hall infuriated me. No one entered my private hospital room until eight the next morning, after I had pissed myself.

By that point, I had worn myself down and didn't even bother acknowledging the shift change. The doctor appeared in the doorway, shaking his head and scribbling on a note pad. I saw the night nurse leave and then return with the morphine. She shot the vial into my arm with one stormy pump. The drug burned through my vein, cleaving its way up my arm and then jumped to burst in my skull. The pain that resonated across my abdomen along the stitches lacing the skin around my pelvis dulled instantly. I drifted back into that fog of illusion, but not before I saw the nurse walk across the room and erase her name from the white board that read, "Hi! My name is _____ and it is my pleasure to care for you." Her name remains an erased blank in my memory.

When I woke again, a woman with magnificent red curls had replaced her. She carefully inspected the IV and steadily depressed the next dose of liquid from her syringe. This time the sensation seeped over me gradually like I was falling and floating at the same time. She held my hand and quietly explained, "Spontaneous abortions are estimated to occur in up to 20% of all pregnancies. First trimester miscarriages are actually very common; most women don't report them at all." She went on to tell me about D&Cs and rupturing ovarian cysts. She couldn't tell me how early the embryo had actually died but assured me that it didn't make it any less traumatic. I muttered something about selling dolls that spontaneously aborted their fetus to prepare little girls. She told me to rest. Her hair blazed beautifully around her, and I distinctly remember craving a cherry Coke before I drifted out again.

Weeks later, after I was released and sentenced to three more months of bed rest at my parents' house, my mother told me I screamed almost every hour the first few days in the hospital. The nurses assured her I wasn't in any more pain because the morphine was doubled. "But I swear you were," my mom said while filing my toenails at the foot of the bed. She looked at me like she expected me to respond, and then continued, "You would just burst from sleep screaming. Then would fall back again, mumbling *his* name."

My mother was careful never to directly talk about him—but I still felt invaded. It was intrusive enough when they stripped me in the ER only to cover me with ice blankets, but somehow this pathetic visual of myself was worse. I felt like she read my private thoughts at my most vulnerable moment. I felt like my body had, once again, betrayed me. Did I mumble or whisper? Was my tone pleading, or worse, begging? Did I say anything besides his name?

When she finished my toes she brought my pills and soup. She also left a folding of clothes on the dresser for when I felt like showering and slipping into something clean. I recognized the fabrics, "When did you stop by my place?" She picked up the pill bottles to return them to the top shelf in the kitchen. "Don't you remember?" She was looking at me skeptically, "On the way home from the hospital. You must have been a bit out of it."

I picked up the spoon and inspected the onion broth. Standing in the doorway, before turning away, she added, "Don't worry, honey. It was spotless."

That night I called him at two in the morning, deliriously out of my head over a long distance phone call. I wanted to tell him how something had broken inside me and how I couldn't repair it. I wanted to tell him about the handle I pulled to sink the red mass and the button I pushed for more morphine. I wanted to tell him how I would wake up alone in the hospital at five in the morning and hear the babies down the hall wailing to be fed and how those babies wouldn't know what a spontaneous abortion feels like until, perhaps, much later in life. But all of those thoughts washed away when I heard his voice sing, "Hello, Sunshine."

The Change
Gigi Rosenberg

One day I realized it had been months.

If the first one meant I was a woman.
What does the last one mean?

So, at 53, I bought the second pregnancy test
I've ever bought.

You never know.

I didn't bother to read the instructions for the test
because, for God's sakes, I'm 53.

Then ended up peeing on the handle and wondering
why no blue lines appeared in two minutes as promised.

I want to change.
I do.
But I'm sad knowing it's over.

My husband and I will never again
sneak into his parents' bathroom
off the kitchen.
We won't watch the pink cross form
confirming my nausea.

He won't say: it's going to be okay.

We won't sit with his parents on the outside patio.
We won't say: we have something to tell you.

His mother won't clap her hand to her mouth.

She, who came all the way from Poland,
who gave up on us after ten years of no babies.

We don't know that in a year
I will stand in the doorway of her room
with the baby in my arms.
His mother, in the hospital bed,
pink puffs of slippers on the floor.
And wave good-bye.

Afraid to go to her bedside.
Knowing that she's leaving soon.
For someplace I don't want to go.
Afraid that even by touching her
I could fall in too.

The Curse Now Lifted
Wendy L. Schmidt

Celia never saw it coming, no matter how many times the warning bells rang, no matter how many ways her body sent up flares and red flags. She'd felt slight flashes, warm currents coursing through her arms and legs, turning her face and ears a hot pink. But she hadn't made the connection. It was really no big secret, no big surprise, this transformation. It had been knocking at her door for months. But, she kept thinking the bad moods were caused by depression. She kept believing the scant days were stress induced. She secretly hoped, in her deepest heart, the skipped months might mean a late-in-life baby boom.

She made an appointment for her yearly dose of reassurance. The Big C was always in the back of her mind as she shivered in her thin gown and placed two feet in the metal stirrups. She chatted nervously about nothing while the doctor probed sensitive spots.

"How long has it been?" the gyno wanted to know. "How many months without—one, two, six?"

Reality hit like a sharp blow when Celia suddenly remembered.

"Two months," she murmured.

"That's not so long," the gyno replied.

"No, you don't understand. I mean two months before my last birthday." That meant more than a year of scant and skips and finally nothing.

"Oh—I see. Well, you're a little young for it. Let's do a blood test to check things out." The doctor poked the needle into a ripe vein and took a vial of blood.

"Check what out?"

"Nothing to worry about. Wait here."

Celia's body felt tight, tense, and trembled from cold and anxiety. Life had been unkind as of late, a slow, painful crash of the last kids leaving home and her husband leaving soon after. She hadn't taken much notice of her body's timetable. There had been whole days when it was all she could do just to get out of bed. Days turned into months, and her cycles were not even on the radar. Now that her head was clearing, it seemed quite possible that they had ended.

She glanced at her watch. Twenty minutes of waiting felt like two hours.

"Where's that damn doctor," Celia grumbled, then picked up an old copy of *People* magazine. Prince William and Kate were on the cover in their wedding apparel. They looked happy and young and ready to start a life of bliss and babies.

I was that girl once upon a time. When did I stop believing in happy endings, she thought.

Celia had become detached from her own body. The seesaw mood swings and intense food cravings, cramps and final flow, had all but disappeared. It had never been easy for her. She often hated the whole damned burden of being female. Still, now that the process was threatened, it was sobering. Was this really the end of youth and the beginning of midlife? Crone, that's what her Wiccan friend called it. She didn't like that word any better than ma'am or old lady.

The doctor entered with a paper in her hands.

"Menopause," she stated. At last the dreaded word was uttered. "According to the test, the worst part is over already. You never noticed any hot flashes or mood swings?"

"Over?" Celia cried. "How can it be over when I didn't even notice the last one?"

"Consider yourself lucky that the symptoms were mild. Many women have to go on hormones just to get through."

The roller coaster ride of waiting, every month, for the fleeting promise or peril of pregnancy was over. Was that lucky? Sometime during the previous two years her body had produced its last, fragile egg. Such a momentous event with no major clue. It hadn't hit her on the head as she'd been warned, awash in sweat and insomnia. Instead, it had disappeared like a thief in the night.

Celia started to cry. Another huge change, and it seemed like the last straw. What was she supposed to do now? No more curse. She laughed a little, feeling slightly silly thinking of the coded phrase her mother had used to describe menstruation.

"It's normal to feel a little loss," the doctor said and patted Celia's hand. "The good news is, since you've passed through, hormones won't be necessary. Your body will feel some additional changes. For instance, I recommend a bit of lubrication for any dryness. You can still enjoy a robust sex life."

"I can't remember the last time I enjoyed a robust sex life," Celia replied and began to laugh even harder. "At my age what chance is there of finding another partner who wants me sexually? Am I technically even a woman anymore? I feel old and cheated, certainly not lucky."

"Perhaps you should consider a different antidepressant," the doctor offered.

"No—no more pills to numb my pain. I've had enough of living in a fog."

Was this the beginning of the end? Or maybe, just maybe, if Celia was brave enough, this could be the beginning of a new freedom. She was single again, still vital, still attractive and slowly finding herself after being defined, for so long, by marriage and motherhood. No more curse, no more cramps, no more murderous monthly moods, no more wifely duties. Her energy might be better spent on other things, and she could redefine herself. Yes, it was another major change but perhaps a welcome one after all.

"Whatever comes I'm going to face it head on. I'm not going to miss out on any more of my life."

Depends
Lois Marie Harrod

As Jim explained when Sara Rubin's call came, his wife couldn't do it because she was teaching a class, so he would. Yes, he would come and get Sara and take her to the grocery store and to Lens Crafters to get her glasses repaired if that's what she needed. Jim was that kind of man.

He had been a retired philosophy professor for six months now, and he was thoroughly enjoying sitting around and reading. Reading was what he had wanted to do, and actually had done, most of his life — reading and thinking, but now he could read and think exactly what he wanted to, when he wanted to. No more keeping up with his subscriptions to *The Journal of Applied Philosophy* and *The Journal of Artificial Intelligence Research* and *The Journal of Beliefs & Values*. He could delve into *Scientific American* and scour *The Wilson Quarterly*, and since they had just traveled to Argentina, more or less obscure Argentinean novelists such as Osvaldo Lamborghini, Victoriano Lillo Catalán, and Benito Lynch. Jim was that kind of man.

Of course, Jim would have rather stayed home and finished Lynch's quirky little gaucho stories with their peculiar magic realism. Still, after his year of reading was up, he planned to do something to save the world, as he liked to say. It was what he and his friends talked about when they got together: how soon they were planning to get off their duffs and do something to better mankind. After all, they did have lots of talents and surely they could volunteer for something.

What that thing was, Jim didn't yet know. Maybe the Peace Corps. Maybe Habitat for Humanity. Maybe the ACLU. But he was pretty sure that it wasn't taking Sara Rubin to Trader Joe's to buy Depends.

His wife Pris was the one who should have made that trip. Pris was a woman, and it wouldn't be so embarrassing for Sara. Besides, Pris was the one who always did things for people.

Pris, to Jim's irritation, seemed to have any number of old ladies who seemed to depend on her to buy them coffee and pick up medicines. When Sara got ovarian cancer, she had become one of Pris' brood. Pris had been running over every so often with hot soup or crackers or soda or whatever she thought Sara might want. But Pris, as she said, wasn't the only one. Sara had a great circle of friends—her literary friends, her scientific friends, her synagogue-going friends, a huge circle. So the burden of Sara's chemo was being distributed around. Today was different. The only one home was Jim.

And now Sara needed Depends because, as she explained in great detail to Jim once she got in the car, the chemo had made her incontinent. "TMI," Jim told Pris later. "Too much information." But that was the kind of person Sara was. A collector of facts and ideas. A former classics professor who had been married to a physicist. "The smartest woman I know," said Pris. "What a memory."

Sara didn't look too good when Jim went to her apartment door. She had lost a lot of weight—62 pounds, she told Jim—and she was wearing an odd sort of tunic under her coat that looked a little like a Navaho nightgown, Jim thought.

"Wanted to wear some color," Sara said. "Needed to cheer myself up."

Jim remembered catching a bit of CNN a year or so ago, when Tammy Faye Messner, of Tammy Faye Bakker TV religion fame, had appeared on the show with Larry King. Such a strange Tammy Faye with a rouged death's head. Sara's makeup looked the same: too much lipstick seeming to wobble off her mouth. She didn't have the Tammy Faye eyelashes now. "My eyelashes fell out," she said to Jim. "And today, I could hardly bare it, my pubic hair. I did not know I would lose my pubic hair."

"TMI," Jim would later again say to Pris. "Too much information."

The bones of Sara's face, which Jim had once thought beautiful, but never mentioned to Pris, were painfully evident. They rode the elevator down, and Sara kept looking up at the mirror trying to adjust her wig. It looked expensive, but it also looked like a wig. The same kinky curly gray frizz Sara had always had, but irremediably not her own. Jim had no idea where one could buy such a thing, but later Pris said Sara had told her all about it, the wig place she had found on the Internet. It was called All Your Own, and what you did was collect your hair as it fell out and when you got a good bunch of it, you sent it off and they had it back to you in less than a week. It was your own hair mixed with hair a lot like your own, a wig. Jim thought Sara looked strange in it somehow, but he couldn't tell exactly why it no longer seemed to be Sara's own. Maybe it was the hair or maybe it was the penciled eyebrows and the hairless eyelids. Even so, Jim tried not to watch Sara's adjustments on the way down. It seemed as if when she adjusted the gray afro, she was trying to flirt with him.

"I am no longer a woman," she told Jim once they got in the car. "That's what I realized, I could no longer conceive of myself as a woman. Maybe that sounds strange to you, a man, but I am not a woman any more. The uterus is gone. The ovaries are gone. I mean where would you be if your penis were gone." Jim didn't know quite how to respond. His years of reading hadn't prepared him for this. He decided it would be best to just watch the traffic and get them to Trader Joe's.

"Having to wear diapers and then running out. What am I? A child not yet toilet trained? A sexless child not yet toilet trained. Well, I guess that is what it is now." She reached out and tapped Jim's wrist on the steering wheel.

"The oncologist took me aside and told me everything I could expect, but he didn't mention this—not incontinence. Isn't that something you'd want to know?"

Jim nodded.

"And now what am I? A husk. A pod in a pair of Depends. As soon as you park, I am heading for that restroom at Trader Joe's. I mean, wouldn't you want to know?"

SELF-DISCOVERY

Midlife Arrhythmias

Marianne Taylor

I. Overture

Music of flute
on an evening beach
or on city walls pre-dawn
A wavering chevron —
now cerulean, now cerise

A skip on water's skin
an intermittent, kicking
breeze, stippling shadows
of birch and fern, printing
mossed banks with motion

Hum in falcon's flight
hungry, uncertain of a catch
in this rush before dark
in the face of a moon
that waxes and wanes

II. Dream

a handsome face shrinks
tan skin morphs to leather
one brown eye clouds milky gray

I had been leaning in to his kiss
already feeling lips, tongue
warm gold hum, like sun on eyelids

just a dream — I draw back
but the monkeyfish stays

I can't tell what he wants to say

III. Grind

Willsmom, Jamesmom, Tomsdad,
tekonyms take over with every mouthful
of candy cereal, box of juice, bag of chips
and bland noodle dinner two hours too early.
Drive the minivan to the mall for Nikes
lose the loose-weave texture of weekends
before soccer, Sunday school, recitals.
Recycle the pristine *Times* again. And again.

Know where to buy neon posterboard
and the name of every leaf in Memorial Park
how many bags of M&M's make 100
and the difference between *grind* and *grind* and *grind*.

Wait. The redemption, mention that.
Yes, hmm. It's not the replication, but the
essential hunger of these temporary children,
their warm breath rising like steam in the dark.

IV. Inheritance

Handed down dreams of
mothers and grandmothers,
humming while they rocked:

Teach, sing, return to the farm,
marry for love.
Live in the city, cut your hair short,
raise perfect children who'll place
flowers on your grave.

Rare noons on the porch, or
late in the sleeping house, I listen.
Their hum, though original as my breath,
is not mine.

Bruised with their yearning
a confusion of ripe desire,
I'm reluctant to imprint.

Salsa plays when I nurse.

V. Sonnet

An ex-mother-in-law's mother's gesture
when faced with features life shouldn't show —

her husband brings home his lover, expects her,
this local diva, raven hair, skin like snow,
to fit right in among the children and servants
have dinner with the family, then pose
in his studio, inspire his waning talents

(his work now features apples on pillows,
plums and figs in a tangle of satin drapery)
sleep in his room with the restless hum of the sea
and rise to join his wife for breakfast, eat
her daily bread in *her* father's house thankfully

—was to raise her hand and smash every mirror
in twenty rooms. Trample the glass on the floor.

VI. Ritual

Gold crusted saints, gaunt and flat,
smoke clouds of incense
chant following chant

vic'naja pamjat, vic'naja pamjat

To march in procession annually
walk up that hill, absorb crowd's hum —
is to know that even for Sisyphus
suffering became habit

Aim to break mine, see anew — alter
experience God by writing it down
despite this leaky pen, debt &
error, so much red ink

VII. Reprise

Like a bell
once rung

altering the air
with its hum

this catch
will hold

and yield

Becoming a Nomad
Patti Capel Swartz

The nomadic subject is a myth, that is to say a political fiction, that allows me to think through and move across established categories and levels of experience: blurring boundaries without burning bridges.
  --Rosi Braidotti, Nomadic Subjects.

When I was a child growing up on a small dairy farm in Ohio, my parents insisted in participation in two spring tasks — stonepicking and mustard pulling. When I was very young, the stones I could lift from the fields to throw into the high spring wagon (a prevention after winter's heaving frosts against the breakage of plowshares) were very small. As I got older, the stones grew in size and weight. It always seemed to me a particularly arduous and endless task, for each year the earth would spew forth more rocks that had to be removed from the fields. I did, however, have some idea of where to begin this task. I simply had to follow the wagon in its progress through the field.

Mustard pulling, on the other hand, seemed to have no beginning and no ending. I would survey the field of emerging oats or wheat, and it would seem that the gracefully waving, taller, yellow-headed stalks of mustard were everywhere. I knew where to begin, but I never seemed to finish, for when I *thought* the field was completed, one of my parents would point out that, while my back was turned, more plants had burst into bloom and needed removal. These two seemingly never-ending tasks are like the tasks of growth and change through which we travel between worlds.

Where I grew up in the 1950s on a small farm in Ohio, few students went on to college. We needed, it was thought, to be filled with basic literacy: the ability in mathematical computation to determine the amount of seed needed for planting, to project the yield per acre, the profit from a bushel of wheat, or to be workers in industry who would follow instructions without question. We needed the ability to read and comprehend enough to keep political structures in place, but not so much that we would begin to question too greatly the existing social and political structures. We were being schooled to be obedient, not to subvert political, economic, and social structures and discourses, to remain in our place. We were taught that all knowledge worth knowing had been discovered, and that we were simply repositories to be filled. Surely, the educational narration that attempted to keep us contained was sick, although deviance from that narrative was characterized by the narrative itself as a form of sickness.

We were fed ideology. We were the first generation of the Atomic Age, and the lessons we learned about atomic power and the destructive force of the atom were tinged with fear. It was this fear that celebrated the "nuclear" family as a retreat and haven for the worker (read man) who had to enter into the commerce of this alienating world. It became increasingly important for us not to question, but rather to listen to the discourses of destruction and power that insisted we obey and continue racism, sexism, and xenophobia. Out of school, the lessons of McCarthyism, the ideology of the Taft-Hartley Act to end railroad and steel strikes "for the good of the country" taught us lessons as well. The good of the country was not always the good of the worker whose well-being must be sacrificed to the greater good, and protest would not necessarily lead to change.

There were contradictions. The arms race that claimed to be our salvation also carried the threat of extinction of the earth, but we were taught, through fear, that its continuation was necessary to prevent the very destruction that it threatened. In the 1950s, women were indoctrinated with cultural messages of their importance in the home: consumerism and "staying home" were glamorized, seen for the national good. This discourse, newly reinforced through the new medium of television, ignored women who had always worked and still worked out of necessity, and the working conditions under which they struggled in canneries, garment sweatshops, cotton mills, as domestic workers, office workers, sales clerks, and field laborers. As farm children, we ignored differences in gender constructions that our mothers demonstrated as workers not only in the house, but in fields and barns. The nuclear family was the "American Dream." Those of us who were different—economically, racially, sexually, or in gender—could not find ourselves represented.

The cultural messages I received told me that I should aspire to be a secretary, a nurse, or a teacher until I married and cared for a family, that I should be ashamed of my working-class background. I should ignore what "they" proclaimed were deviant differences in my sexuality and gender to maintain the norms of heterosexuality and domesticity. Working-class and non-traditional women remained all but invisible in media culture as I was growing up. Working-class women increasingly internalized messages of shame for their own failure to move into the middle class.

In high school I first really examined the constructions of "race." The rural community in which I grew up was almost entirely "white" and most families were farmers. Most students were "white." Two African American students, a brother and sister, and several children of a "mixed-race" family attended the school. Their social isolation and exclusion was almost complete. The son of the "mixed race" family who was in almost all of my college preparatory classes could find no one to date, almost no one with whom to study, because of both race and class, despite his efforts to fit in. I was aware of his plight, sympathetic to it, but scared to death to lose my own shaky standing as a working-poor lesbian masquerading as a straight, middle-class student. The young African American woman was both my friend (although describing our relationship as a friendship does not describe the alterity and separateness of our relationship) and a threat to the fiction I had created of my existence. Smarter than most of the white elite, more middle class in income than most of the white students, she was in few activities and certainly not one of those tapped for membership in the National Honor Society, as I was despite my poverty. From her marginalized position in the society of the school, Sandra was the one person I felt saw behind my masquerade. She saw that I did not really fit in any better than did she. But she also recognized that I was too much of a coward, too afraid of exposing who I really was, to really engage her in friendship.

In college I found my own marginalized group: theatre people. In a university that primarily dedicated itself to the production of teachers, we in theatre were on the outside. This gave me freedom to change some of my perceptions of race and friendships across racial boundaries. Although I was still afraid to admit my lesbianism, I could at least become friends across lines of race and culture, and I began to learn a little about constructions of race and power.

During the last year of classes, I attended college part time and worked full time at my first real job as a caseworker at what was then called the Welfare Department. Entering the world of my casework district, I entered a bordered country. In this world, the American Dream was questioned daily by the inhabitants who were denied access to it. This was the place where I learned that borderlands exist: an inner-city ghetto where cultures mixed, sometimes blended, more often clashed. Here I learned that cities existed within cities and cultures within cultures. My casework area was between ten and twenty square blocks, an area now flattened by urban renewal: the streets once teeming with life looked like nothing so much as a bombed-out city of vacant lots gone to weeds. As Thulani Davis points out in *1959*, urban renewal was designed to break communities and prevent protest.

My own position as representative of colonist oppression was made clear to me by a young woman determined to make a better life for her son. Determined to get off welfare, she had obtained a position as a nurse's aide. When I had to terminate her benefits, she telephoned, angry and hostile, screaming at me of the injustice of her position, her punishment (which I could not deny), for attempting to improve hers and her son's living conditions. Both of us caught in the discourses of poverty and racism, she could only rail at me as a representative of policies that strangled her efforts for change, and I could only listen sympathetically to what I knew was true of her life.

It was 1965 turning to 1966, a time of great unrest and anger. There was increasing awareness of aspects of race in the Vietnam War where young black men who could not afford to avoid the draft were being killed in great numbers fighting a war against people of color. If lucky enough to survive, these men were returning home to hostility because the messages of the nightly news were being sent to the white American public that the men of color returning were now trained revolutionaries to be feared. Civil unrest and violence were treated by the media as new events, ignoring the history of civil unrest and protest that has long been a part of and outgrowth of racial and class constructions in this country.

Later, as an employment counselor, then an adoption recruiter and a resident counselor, I would learn much more about the ways in which the law punishes and disenfranchises people who inhabit borderlands, and it punishes difference. I would see children who were difficult to place because of race; children who were removed from their homes because those homes or parents would not conform to the white, middle-class norms, or because the parents dared to critique the system, speaking out for the rights of the family, only to have their children removed.

My life experiences have led me to question what it means to be white in a society that privileges whiteness. How is my life as a white woman constructed differently than the life of a woman of color? In what ways has privilege made me blind? How does race interfere with coalition forming? How do I find the information that will allow me to become what philosopher and theorist Maria Lugones calls a "world-traveler": to see from multiple perspectives, to attempt to form coalitions, to enrich my life? Can I help to construct a more equitable world?

When I left the area where I had grown up and the family that was almost grown to attend graduate school, I entered a kind of exile. Exile, traveling between and among worlds, whether enforced or self-imposed, can be a way of finding the self and of constructing and narrating changing stories. Exile and the subsequent nomadism that so often follows its institution demands the construction of new and/or revised stories of life and experience because altered living conditions preclude the sense of the stories with which one once constructed one's life. The exile and/or the nomad, through changing living situations and changing perceptions, recognizes the narrative nature of experience and translates that experience through continual revision of that narrative in relation to community. Creating narrative, whether the construction of the personal stories that one lives by or the construction of stories through oral or written art, is an integral part of living and becoming.

When I attempted to make my story fit within the contextual confines of a static social order, I found myself doubled: two narrators, one watching from a detached distance as the other performed social and narrative acts that allowed her to fit within what she saw as belonging; the observing self giving lie to stasis but without the necessary internal or imposed courage to attempt a transformational narrative. Over half of the life I have lived was narrated in this way, the "outside" narrator a cynical observer and storyteller, looking for permanency, for closure to gain comfort. Mine is not an uncommon story. Not fitting within the confines of traditional contextual narrations is a commonality of those who, for sexual, racial, social, or political reasons, exist outside of mainstream narratives, rocks standing out of the creekbed around which the water swirls.

This exiled or outsider self is, I think, the reason I was early attracted to acting. Performing an identity allowed me the freedom to explore and to try on other identities: to enter imaginatively into other worlds; to be a world-traveler. Performing also created questions about the nature and fixity of reality. Multiple interpretations of the same story were possible, and even desirable: even if there was closure in the writing or the play, performance itself had no closure. Each performance was slightly altered through audience response, through the interaction of the actors, and through nuances in interpretation.

The exile and/or the nomad, through changing living situations and changing perceptions, recognizes the narrative nature of experience and translates that experience through continual revision of that narrative in relation to community.

Exile requires translation. Translation of language, social, political, racial, sexual, and gender construction often makes a reevaluation of one's personal story necessary as the constants or givens of a life that no longer make sense, taken out of the context in which they were previously narrated. Translation from one life or one set of experiences to another becomes not only a way of making sense of stories and re-visioning events, but it often also acts as resistance to and rewriting of the dominant discourse and to creating resistance to closure. When I decided to change my geophysical location, I moved to California for a specific purpose — working toward a degree. Although the position of student is a privileged one and although I benefitted greatly from white privilege, I did not feel particularly privileged at the time, for to attempt to make ends meet I attended classes full time, and I worked both full-time and part-time jobs. With at least fifty hours a week in employment before classes, I was exhausted much of the time and often still without money, sometimes fed by neighbors in the *barrio* community in which I lived: neighbors who could not reasonably afford to do this, but who felt that friendship required such generosity.

During that period while I examined my life and tried to see some future, and in subsequent moves to Georgia and Kentucky, I entered the life of a nomad, increasingly understanding that my home is in myself, that I carry my life with me, and that change not only allows for transformation and subjective and theoretical repositioning, but also allows for entrance into many worlds. The need to obtain permanency and security diminished with the realization that neither exist, that they are not *real* but only *reified constructions of conceptual language*. The nomad discovers that new people with different customs and different perspectives are open to friendliness, to sharing perspectives and subjectivities, and to engaging with the stories and constructions that the nomad brings as well as performing their own sharing. I am reminded of Jacqueline Mirsadeghi's photograph entitled *Passages vers l'infini,* in which the subject is a series of open doorways, staircases, and passages leading in many directions, some shadowed, but with the promise of light in more than one direction. Indeed, the promise of movement and light lead the eye and the imagination into these passages that indicate a state of becoming.

A geographical move often interrupts the story we have understood and told ourselves, causing us to interrogate and make changes in the narration of our lives. Writer Sandra Cisneros, for instance, speaking at a 1992 Modern Language Association Convention session, said that a move to Texas had given her a landscape that fit her mind. However, as writer Dorothy Allison has said, a move that changes perspectives need not be geographical, but "you have to get distance, you have to go away in your head" in order to see and narrate a story or stories from differing perspectives (personal communication March 25, 1994).

The change in landscape can be physical or a change of the landscape of the mind. I became a chameleon, and only when this behavior became life threatening did I gain the courage to attempt to change that behavior. The narration of my life within acceptable social and political contexts had become too uncomfortable to endure. I was exiled from myself. I exiled myself to save my life. By drastically changing the contexts of my life, I was able to develop a narrative that allowed me to see possibilities for world traveling.

Exile is possible with or without geographical movement. Exile has been a part of my entire remembered life: I don't remember ever feeling as though I fit into the contexts in which I lived until recently. "Coming home" from exile for me was realizing that there was no truth, no static center, but that rather I live in constant transformation and narration of changing stories, a narrative that constitutes an ever-changing self: I live in myself as a woman. Creating distance and changing perspectives free women to think in a way that permits the speaking of "the unspeakable." Women can become, in the words of philosopher Maria Lugones, "world-travellers."

Works Cited

Allison, Dorothy. Personal Communication. March 21, 1994. Columbia, South Carolina.

Braidotti, Rosi. *Nomadic Subjects: Embodiment and Sexual Difference in Contemporary Feminist Theory.* New York: Columbia University Press, 1994.

Cisneros, Sandra. Reading at The Modern Language Association Convention, New York, December, 1992.

Davis, Thulani. *1959: A Novel.* New York: HarperCollins, 1992.

Lugones, Maria. "Playfulness, 'World'-Travelling, and Loving Perception.'" In *The Woman That I Am.* Ed.D.

Soyini Madison. New York: St. Martins, 1994.

Mirsadeghi, Jacqueline. *Passages vers l'infini.* Musée de l'Elysée, Lausanne. News Productions, CH-1446 Baulmes 55536.

Swartz, Patti Capel. "An Interview with Dorothy Allison." *The Sojourner.* November, 1994. pp. 8,9.

Mamie's Grocery

Loren Hecht

To get to Mamie's Grocery in Tower Gardens you had to make the slow and dangerous trek over vast and terrifying neighborhood terrain. The store was located only three blocks away from where I lived, but to me, a seven-year-old tomboy, tiny and worrisome, frightened of everything, the journey to Mamie's seemed terrible and immense, wild and impossible and ominous.

The summer of 1964 was hot. A hot, sweltering, fat pigeon summer. The summer after John F. Kennedy was assassinated. The summer the Beatles invaded. The summer after the October Missile Crisis when my mother built the bomb shelter downstairs. It was squeezed into a closet in the basement, beneath the steps. A big closet, rigged up with nothing to keep radiation out, but enough food and water to last ten years. There were innumerable tin cans on innumerable shelves. Row upon row, shelf upon shelf, tin cans like books, archives of tin, shimmery and silver with bright labels — Campbell's Chicken Soup, Delmonte Pears, Heinz Tomato Paste, Log Cabin Syrup, Mott's Applesauce, Skippy Peanut Butter. And beans: lentil beans, pinto beans, kidney beans, string beans, lima beans, black beans, green beans, jelly beans. Beans and beans and beans and beans and beans and.... In 1964, people were scared. My parents were scared. Those late-night conversations with the neighbors in the kitchen, all strained and dark, undertoned and choked down, heavy adult talk I wasn't supposed to listen in on, with words and phrases beyond my peeping-tom comprehension. "Bay of Pigs," "Iron Curtain," "Sputnik."

As for me, at seven years old I had more important things to think about, like getting to Mamie's. All I ever wanted was to get to Mamie's.

Mamie's Grocery in Tower Gardens was a paradise; it was ecstasy; the land of Oz, hope and light and possibility. Ballard's butterscotch bars in big barrels, monster tubs you could dive in to. Sweitzer's licorice whips wrapped in spirals around cornstalk tall metal pipes. Mammoth pretzels dipped in Hershey's dark chocolate, sold out of huge copper buckets. Mickey Mouse balloons, sidewalk chalk, cats-eye marbles, the place had everything. Balsa wood, BB bullets, paddle balls, pop-guns, comic books, and "Snakes" — those centimeter long charcoal cylinders — light one up at the top—wheeeeeeze!— sold in miniature finger boxes. My pennies always turned into Bazookas. Sometimes I'd sit on top of the Coca-Cola cooler, bust out a Bazooka, and read through the comic wrapper while chewing. "What's 'le Bazooka Joe doin' today?"

A little bell on a coil above the door sang out when you walked in. Ringy ding! Ringy ding! Ding a ling, ding a ling, ding a ling. Candy time!

Mamie, behind the counter, always watched you walking in. She was a big woman. Huge. Six, seven, eight foot in ratty slippers, pink colored, threadbare things she never took off. She had a big fat belly and a real small, not quite grown-in head; like a single scoop with a cherry on top. Her bosoms were big as beach balls. And her teeth were all over the place, short, stubby chicklettes. Her popeyes were eightballs set in pockets of blubber. And they were wet, perpetually soggy and wet; threatening, like "The Sucking Field" behind John Sears' house. What scared me most about Mamie was her mouth. A big, gaping cavernous maw around which she smeared a jellylike substance. Sticky looking. Semi-congealed blood pudding. Her voice had a kind of rumble to it, a kind of outrageous thick rasp. She smoked all the time, Lucky Strikes, like a chimney. Her voice was gangster farts pushed through burnt vocal cords. Guttural and low down, the sound of cruelty and intolerance. "CAN... I... HELP... YOU!"

It was on a Tuesday afternoon I decided to take a walk to Mamie's.

I was playing in my bedroom, balls and jacks. That was my game, balls and jacks. I was neighborhood champ. Even outside, I could swipe the plate of the sidewalk clean every time without once bloodying my palms.

I heard my mother calling me.

"Honey, why don't you go outside and get some fresh air."

My brothers were away at camp. And John Sears, my best friend, was off visiting his aunt and uncle in the Adirondacks. I had nowhere to go outside. Nothing to do. Wait. What about Mamie's? No, too dangerous. Not alone. Why not? You could run the whole way, sneak out the back, don't tell mom. No, not alone. Too dangerous. Go. Go to Mamie's...

I found my money where I kept it, in a shoebox beneath my bed. Three quarters, two dimes, seventeen pennies. Go. Fast. Run the whole way.

I raced to the kitchen, pocketed a chocolate chip Tollhouse, kissed my mother on the cheek, then dashed out the back door; past my mother's planted petunias, roses, lilacs, and perennials in full bloom; past my mother's flower garden, to the edge of the silent woods behind our house. I stood, alone, staring up into dense forest (the single row of corkscrew willows behind our house) a density of branches and hanging vines, nooses ready to lynch me should I accidentally step into the trap. Zoop! Snap! Snare grabs child's leg. Snap! Lift. Downside up. Upside down. One dead child hanging from a tree. D...Y...I...I...I...N...G... I had to walk cautiously, carefully. Watch your step! Watch your step! I could hear the chop caw of crows in the distance. I'd seen a crow once eat the raw guts out of a dead squirrel. Watch your step! Watch your step! I tiptoed cautiously through, twig to twig, leaf to leaf. The woods smelled of pinecones, hickory bark, and the razor heat of summer.

Suddenly, pop! I was out of the woods and staring mute and dazed into an immense mountainous wasteland. "The Cliffs" — unimpressive dirt mounds to the average adult — but to me, fantastic ascending crags requiring great courage to scale.

I felt thirsty, horribly, unnaturally and suddenly thirsty. I scanned the terrain. This was an easy place to die in. You sprain your ankle. You can't walk. You die of thirst. Your body goes undiscovered for months. A desiccated wisp. It crumbles into the sand. I took the cliffs one step at a time, slowly, carefully, thirsty. Frightened of the sun.

At last, I found myself in Mrs. Schmidt's backyard staring up at monster sunflowers planted intentionally to eat small children alive — THERE'S SCHMIDT! SHE SEES US!

MAKE A RUN FOR IT!

I launched quickly away and found myself ankle deep in the field behind John Sears' house; "The Sucking Field," made of mud and straw balled up and engorged in riverly spills of cloudy water. A crater and water choked acre of land (which was in reality no acre at all, but twenty feet of Mrs. Sears' turnip patch). WATCH OUT! NIGHT SNAKE MIGHT SWALLOW YOU UP! EAT YOU ALIVE! MAKE A RUN FOR IT! I could feel it, "The Sucking Field" grabbing at me, clawing at me, sucking me down and into the bowels of the earth. I considered turning back.

Suddenly, bam! I burst free of the killing field and was flying flying flying across vacant neighborhood sidewalk, covered over with chalk games, four square and hopscotch; past Nora Barson's backyard, where it was said the old man lost his ear from frost bite; up and over the road, onto the Whitehills school playground: a derangement of slides and bars, planks and hard plastic. Iron, metal, and steel in a confusion of parts, summoning children to climb up, summoning me to climb up, up, and over the earth where things are wet and suck you down.

At last, I found myself before the dividing wall that separated my neighborhood, Whitehills, from the neighboring community, Tower Gardens, ominous, bleak, deadly.

"They'll suck the marrow out of your bones with a straw," John Sears used to tell me.

"The TG's want revenge, they hate Whitehills. They're killers. Killers!"

The houses looked intentionally cruel and isolated. Some of them boarded up. Others in disrepair. Semi-completed structures made of basement space with a flat roof on top, scalped bunkers out of which the inhabitants no doubt took aim through low windows, sniper houses in camouflage.

I made it to the tree opposite "Dead-Man's Curve," that curve of stories, severed heads, and bloodied stumps.

"People crash in TG, and nobody gives a care," John Sears used to tell me.

My senses alert, I strode feverish, pitched, edgy.

Suddenly, BANG! My legs exploded out from under me.

BANG BANG BANG! Electricity tore through me.

BANG BANG BANG. Make a run for it!

BANG BANG BANG BANG BANG! Bullets in my back. I went down.

I awakened in what seemed to be a spongelike substance, couch of slow foam, cotton candy without the textured filament. Physical generosity. "I'm dead," I thought. John Sears was right. The TG's got revenge.

I slowly opened my eyes.

Monster! Vorgon! Horror! Cyclops! Big-eyed, bulge-eyed, monster-eyed, horrible murdering Mamie! I was laying in Mamie's arms!

I did not have the strength enough to fight back. I just lay there, awaiting my fate. Would she ball me up, shove me inside her greedy mouth, eat me alive?

"Look what you done now, Hoover! Get out of that ole Jalopy, come over here and apologize to this little girl," Mamie said.

A spindly man came walking toward us. He stood before Mamie and humbly apologized to me, bowing slightly, a very odd appearance.

"That backfiring hunk of junk is a menace to the neighborhood and my business!" Mamie told the man. He apologized again. He'd have the thing looked at.

Obviously, the two of them were in cahoots. I could see that. Should I let down my guard now, BOOM! she'd swallow me whole.

"You really whelped it up good." She was talking to me now. Strange. Her voice sounded softer than usual, not scratchy like before. Grandmotherly, with a nasally cold in her sinuses.

Mamie shifted my weight in her fleshy arms and cradled me closer to her. She smelled of fresh cut firewood, peeled oranges, bazooka bubble gum.

"You almost gave me a heart attack with all that yellin!" she told me. I saw the pulley of her jaw tug open. Little boxcar teeth peep out. Her wet eyes seemed less like "The Sucking Field" more like sad rain on glass. I let down my guard a little.

"How's it now with you, child? How's about a coke? Coke sound good? Let's go inside."

From up high atop Mamie's chariot arms I could see everything. Daisies and dandelions were in bloom all over. Friendly neighbors were talking on open summer porches. Little children were running through sprinklers. A collection of monarchs were dancing in a playful, circular pattern around a bucket of nails.

People and wild things were everywhere. Together.

Spring '69

Ronna Magy

You find yourself running along with the crowd, footsteps pounding as they hit the ground. Past classical buildings inside which only moments before you'd studied the Paris Commune and the French Revolution. Inside those stone walls, behind those glass windows, at those wooden desks, you and others like you, picked up notebook and pen, reflected, and wrote. It is the time of the Vietnam War, during which native mothers burned by napalm carry dead babies in arms along unpaved roads, while male friends take drugs or move to Canada escaping the draft.

Above the crowd now, in the cloudless blue sky of an early spring day, a tear gas canister is hurled. Watching its spin, you estimate where the projectile will land. Quickly, you smear your friend Ruth's Vaseline over cheeks and lips, and for a split second, consider which way to run, north or south.

This semester, the administration announced in the *Daily Californian* that there have been too many demonstrations against the war, too many classes canceled during the student strike. Now the university is reclaiming their buildings, classrooms, students, and land. On this otherwise perfect day, on which a professor is speaking at the north end of campus about ending the war, the university calls out the Berkeley police. An official's bullhorn punctures the silent air announcing, "This is an unlawful assembly. You are ordered to disperse!"

Just above, a canister is hurled, and from out its back end as it lands, a plume of acrid brown smoke penetrates the air. Panic engulfs the crowd that gathered moments ago to listen, now they run screaming as tear gas permeates eyes and skin. Plastic-shielded and blue uniformed, the police begin to fan out and attack. Students disperse inside buildings, places they hope to be safe.

Only a few days ago your friend Debi commented, "We need love, not war," the two of you standing next to the fountain on Sproul Plaza, it was almost midday. A day like this, not a cloud in the sky. A day for a walk down a tree-lined road. A few feet away someone sang, "You masters of war. You that build the big guns," while sandled students and long-haired professors debated Vietnam. "Young lives sacrificed to an old men's war," a paisley-scarved professor told a friend. And her companion agreed, "Another generation lost! And for what?"

Now, alarm fills the air. Students scream. Now, feet run in all directions escaping irritated eyes and skin. Your eyes burn and tear. Newspaper images of napalmed bodies and coffins draped in American flags again sear your mind. Nighttime images that take away dreams. How many more bodies in wooden coffins will come home dead?

Heading south, the two of you pass the fountain, that same fountain, dry and waterless now, and Sproul Plaza, where in '65 Mario and Bettina admonished students to stop this war, stop all wars. The patio so jammed that day, no one could move. Your voices join others in chanting, "No more war. No more war." Fists in the air, the crowd yells, "1-2-3-4 we don't want your fucking war." Over and over, the words repeat, the voices swell. What will it take to stop this war?

Your feet run with the crowd, past student union steps, where just days ago speakers talked of Nixon's War and the money corporations were making mining tin and tungsten in Indo-China, Phil Ochs leading the crowd in, "I Ain't Marching Any More." You run south toward Telegraph hoping to escape the police onslaught and hide amongst the dealers and craftspeople whose booths line the avenue.

At the south end of campus, another police line walls you in. Plastic-shielded and blue uniformed, the police stand en masse, hands ready at their guns. With access to Telegraph blocked, no one can move. The crowd chants, "Hell no, we won't go," forcing itself up against the wall of police. Some are beaten back and dragged off. "Pigs," a young man near you taunts.

In front of the crowd, the blue line of police, behind the crowd, the smoke of tear gas fills the air. Around you, thousands protesting the war. Some sing, "We can see through your masks."

Everyone coughing, the tear-gassed air is difficult to breathe. The police captain bellows into his bullhorn, "This is an illegal gathering. You are all under arrest." The police move in with batons, begin hitting and arresting demonstrators. Some are screaming and stumbling. Some taken off to paddy wagons nearby.

Looking back over your shoulder, you recall the steps that run behind the student union onto a plaza below. "Let's go this way," you yell to Ruth, as the two of you press back into the crowd. Some grope their way down the steps to a landing, to find an open space in the tear-gas filled air. From this plaza below, before police reinforcements arrive, everyone scatters, dispersing to safety along Bancroft and into the Berkeley streets and the world beyond. You are safe there for the moment, until the next demonstration, the next student strike, and the next protest against the war. It is the spring of 1969.

Tiergarten
Susan Winstead

So far, the visit to Berlin had been pleasant. I'd been stationed in West Germany for several years, enjoying a satisfying career as an Army officer.

A shift in policy provided women of my generation the opportunity to serve in the military alongside men. So, I took advantage of this change and served in a force that defended the West from what lie beyond the Wall in the East.

The East German government had built the wall separating East and West Berlin in 1961 to stop the flow of Eastern European refugees. Even though access between East and West had been heavily fortified by concrete and wire and checkpoints named Alpha, Bravo, and then Checkpoint Charlie, people from the West could visit East Berlin.

Change had come to the divided city of Berlin though. Change so significant that the Soviet empire that had captured East Berlin in 1945 had lost its grip affecting political powers and their militaries throughout the world; people took down the Berlin Wall in November 1989.

When this happened, I'd been assigned to a unit in West Germany. So, the following spring I allowed myself a weekend to wander away from my duty station in Frankfurt to see for myself the change that had come to Berlin.

I looked through the window of the tour bus, eager to venture on either side of the now open wall in Berlin. The bus took us to an area where we would be in walking distance to spend the beautiful, fresh spring day at either the Berlin Zoo, shopping at the expensive, modern stores, or wandering the maze of flea market vendors. Having a passion for not only old treasures but also the thrill of the hunt to find a bargain, I opted for the flea market.

The tour guide pointed me in the direction I needed to go. She told me to follow the signs saying *flohmarkt,* the German word for flea market. I would find one near a train station called *Tiergarten.*

I followed the path marked by signs and found the flea market easily, marveling at its size. This flea market was not just one street, but several, creating a maze the size of a football field. I quickly joined the bustle of people to look for a treasure, my bargain. I soon became dumb-struck at what I saw as I inspected the goods for sale.

Antique furniture in mint condition and clothes, racks and racks of vintage clothing worn in an era long ago, caught my attention. Several vendors displayed hundreds of old-fashioned coffee grinders, many with coffee beans, rotting but still recognizable, sitting in them. It seemed as if someone had been in the process of grinding them, then stopped, never to return to the coffee grinder again.

Boxes and boxes of letters written in longhand overflowed on table tops, some falling to the ground. The envelopes and paper had yellowed so badly I could barely read the writing in the German language. Primarily though, the countless leather bound photo albums perplexed me. I looked through the pages at pictures of well-dressed men, women, and children. I did not know very much about the history of fashion, especially in Germany, but I guessed the pictures to have been taken sometime from 1900 up to just before World War II. The portraits of families, children, and young women wearing wedding attire made me stop.

Something was very wrong with this flea market. It was too personal.

Who would allow their family heirlooms to be sold on the street to strangers? I felt as if my stomach did a somersault when I noticed that the names on the letters and in the photo albums were Jewish.

While growing up, I had been taught in school about the horrors of World War II. I chose, though, to comfortably steer away from books, movies, and other memorials like the concentration camps. I knew the Holocaust had been wrong, senseless, and horrible, and I kept it at that.

I took a few steps back and stood at the bottom of an earthy incline where at the top lay a railroad track. There were hundreds of people before me browsing from table to table. They apparently did not question the source of all these items.

I thought about my family back in the United States, my brothers and sisters, parents and grandparents, aunts, uncles, and cousins. If we had all been taken from our homes, never to return, what would become of our household property, especially fifty years later? Though it sickened me to think about it, the answer lay obvious before me in living reality.

It was then I noticed the man next to me. He wore brown, corduroy pants and a dark plaid shirt. His mustache and beard heavily covered his face. I said nothing as he looked directly into my eyes and seemed to understand my gaze.

He spoke English well, but I could tell it was not his first language. "So much change," he said. "The Nazis took it, then the Communists kept it. The wall is gone and now free enterprise."

His tone of voice did not sound sarcastic or sympathetic, just matter of fact. He was gone, almost as quickly as when I first noticed him next to me, disappearing into the crowd.

I still think about this man, illusive now, but very real then. It seems as if he was at that place, at that moment to confirm my suspicion.

I abandoned my search for the bargain I had sought that day. Still, I will never forget *Tiergarten*, an experience I did not want or expect, but one that will stay with me forever.

Who Will Remember Hannah Waring?
Nancy Poling

I leaned over the railing of the Burco Mariner and vomited into the Pacific Ocean. It wasn't the gruel I'd eaten for breakfast. No disease was causing me to wretch and moan in agony. No rolling waves were pitching the freighter back and forth.

I was soul sick.

Hannah, you're made of tougher stuff than this, Lowell whispered in my mind. I remember when you'd work out in the field with the men, heaving bales of hay, the time we all lifted a tractor off of Jimmy Matteson. And now you're quitting because of one woman?

My decision has nothing to do with strength or weakness, I said back to him. I'm leaving Korea because…because…oh, I don't know.

I never told them, the board that interviewed me to make sure I was morally and mentally fit. Seated alone at the end of a conference table, answering their questions about my beliefs and how I would handle hardship, I convinced them I was going for the right reasons: to take a message of hope to a war-torn country. They did not recognize what family and friends in Ohio knew: I was not a young woman of deep faith but one whose plans for the future had been disrupted, one with no other idea what to do.

I'd convinced myself that it was Lowell's spirit calling me. While I could not crawl through the mud, burdened with C-rations, a gun, and ammunition, while I would never know what it felt like to come face to face with a thousand Chinese soldiers suddenly appearing over the crest of the mountain, in winter I would experience the bone-chilling cold he had complained about. In summer I would get soaked by monsoon rains and bitten by mosquitoes.

As if Lowell's letters were scripture, I'd spent hours rereading and memorizing them, holding in my heart an image of a young man who couldn't even bring himself to kill an injured farm animal. "Last night it got down to thirty below zero, and I was too cold to sleep. At such times, to ease my mind, I picture that little bungalow on Everett Street, the one with black shutters and ivy climbing the wall, and imagine it is our home. I picture our children, a boy named Junior and a girl named Alice, she with dark hair and eyes like yours. He, of course, like me, except instead of being so serious he laughs a lot. That's what I dream of, dearest. Our future together."

The future that never got to be. The bungalow I would never live in. The children I would never have. No, I said nothing to the committee about Lowell and about the most profound loss of my young life.

Two months of orientation and language study did not prepare me for Seoul. Though the war had been over for nearly five years, there were still piles of rubble in every block, malnourished people searching for food and a place to live. Destruction and poverty everywhere I looked. Yet the physical appearance of women who came to the mission's Social Welfare Center—a two-story Western-style building paid for by American contributions—offered scant evidence of the hardships they faced. Most wore Western clothes: simple skirts and blouses. Clean and carefully ironed.

A new woman showed up at the center. Attractive, not much older than I. Her shoulder-length straight black hair was pulled back and held in place by a ribbon matching her blouse. Three times a week she attended the class for young mothers, sitting alongside everyone else on red and yellow floor cushions. But unlike other women attending, she carried no infant in a quilted *podaeki*; neither did she appear to be pregnant. For three months she came regularly, practiced washing Alice, the rubber doll, in the plastic bathtub, listened to me, a young Western woman who'd never had children, take on an air of expertise about sanitation and immunization.

One day she lingered after class. "I-reum-i-eo-tteo-k'e toe-se-yo?" I asked. (What is your name?)

The woman's gaze remained downward. "Lee Hyun-eun."

"Do you have a child?"

"Yes."

"A son or daughter?"

Lee Hyun-eun made no reply.

Assuming my Korean had not been clear enough, I asked again, "A son or daughter?"

In response, she bowed from the shoulders and turned toward the door.

Aboard the Burco Mariner only Gladys Weimer and I still remained at the Captain's table. Gladys, a missionary returning to the States on furlough, leisurely took nibbles from a piece of chocolate cake while a member of the kitchen staff cleared the few remaining dishes. I sat where I'd earlier forced myself to eat a few crackers and soup.

With a stick figure and fine auburn hair that stuck out in multiple directions, Gladys was probably no more than fifty, yet to me, still in my twenties, she seemed old and wise.

"You're thinking too much like a Westerner," she said after I told her why I was heading home after only eight months. "An American mother thinks in terms of *my* son, *my* daughter. A Korean child belongs to the extended family, the clan."

"But a woman carries the baby inside her for nine months," I insisted. "She has a special relationship with it. If I had a child…"

Gladys turned her ear as if assuming she'd misheard. "Pardon?"

For the first time since leaving home less than a year earlier, I spoke about Lowell. "After he was killed, I wished we'd gotten married before he left, that I had a child, his child."

Gladys took the last bite of cake, chewed it thoughtfully, then daubed at her mouth with the linen napkin.

"I think, dear, that you confused the woman's needs with your own."

The daily five A.M. service. Prayers in Korean. A sermon in Korean. Everything requiring a concentration I lacked energy for so early in the morning. Instead, I directed thoughts to Lowell about the likely day ahead: work at the center, a potluck dinner that evening with other missionaries. I was startled from my reverie as the congregation stood and began robustly singing in Korean:

At the cross, at the cross where I first saw the light.
And the burden of my heart rolled away.
It was there by faith I received my sight,
And now I am happy all the day.

As I started to leave the sanctuary, I saw that Lee Hyun-eun was there too. Our gazes met, and I walked toward her.

"Are you at peace?" I asked in greeting.

Probably because I was teacher, she a pupil, she gave me a shallow bow. "Yes."

But I could tell by the sadness in her eyes that she was not really at peace, and I could feel Lowell steering me to remain beside her.

"I do not see you at church on Sunday mornings," I said.

"My husband does not allow it."

"But you are here now."

"He is still asleep and will not miss me." She paused. "If I become a Christian, will your Jesus make me happy all the day?"

"Yes," I promised, realizing as soon as I said it that my own experience of loss did not support the assurance with which I spoke.

The women filed out of the infant and childcare class, their animated chatter echoing in the hallway. Again, Lee Hyun-eun lingered.

"Please say prayers for me," she said, urgency in her voice. She bent her knees as if to kneel.

"You mean right now?"

"Yes."

Since Lowell's death I'd found no solace in praying, but how could I explain that to Lee Hyun-eun? As the two of us knelt on the hard classroom floor, I struggled to pray in Korean: "Ha-na-nim, you know Lee Hyun-eun, you know and understand the sadness in her heart...."

"I want to be baptized," she said when the prayer ended.

That is how I came to make what you might say was my only convert.

White bare walls, a dusty chalkboard, thin cushions the women had stacked in the corner as they left the room. About to carry my props back to the office, I stood holding Baby Alice and the plastic washtub, a bottle sterilizing pot inside it.

Lee Hyun-eun looked accusingly into my eyes. "I was baptized, but I am not happy all the day."

"What makes you so sad?" I asked. She took the tub and sterilizing pot from my arms, leaving me holding only the rubber Baby Alice as we walked down the hall.

"My son lives with my husband's brother."

"Why is that?"

Lee Hyun-eun hesitated as if doubting whether she should tell me. "My husband's brother is the eldest son. He has only daughters."

"Who makes such a decision?"

"The family council."

"But why?"

I had to lean toward her to hear her soft voice: "So that my husband's older brother will have an eldest son."

"You had to give your boy to your brother-in-law?"

Lee Hyun-eun bit her lip and nodded. I held Baby Alice more tightly, as if I might be required to give her away.

"Where does your brother-in-law's family live?" I asked.

"Near Taejon."

"Is that where you are from?"

"Yes, but there was no work for my husband there....Why did you promise that your Jesus would make me happy all the day?"

I had no answer.

❖

117

Unlike Korean tables, low and close to the heated floor, the kitchen in the single-women's missionary residence had the kind of table and chairs used stateside. As we did most evenings, Martha, Lois, Adelaide, and I gathered there, wearing chenille robes and house slippers. While a heating tea kettle burped on the apartment-size stove nearby, Martha stood, vigorously brushing Lois' long brown hair in preparation for setting it in pin curls. Adelaide, feet propped on the chair Martha had vacated, folded church bulletins for the following Sunday. I just sat there.

"I don't see how this country is ever going to progress," Martha said, holding bobby pins between her teeth. "You know the two Chong brothers—some family event comes along, and they think they should get the time off work."

"Their father's sixtieth birthday," Adelaide said. "A milestone year. And Sung Min's the oldest son. He wouldn't dare miss it."

"Why's that?" I asked. "What's so special about sons? If our fathers had—"

"My dad wanted a boy," Martha said. "Mama's third pregnancy, and out I popped. He decided to treat me like one anyway, taught me to take a car engine apart and put it back together."

"And thanks to him we all have bicycles that work," Adelaide said.

Lois reached up and grabbed Martha's hand. "Ouch, take it easy. That's my scalp you're poking."

"This woman keeps coming to my childcare class," I said. "She's not pregnant, though, and comes alone. Turns out she has a son, but had to give him to her husband's older brother. Something about the brother only having girls."

Martha wrapped a strand of Lois' hair around her index finger. "Maybe because daughters marry and become part of their husband's family. If there's no son, who's going to bring a wife back to take care of the parents in their old age?"

I got up, poured boiling water into the teapot, and carried the pot to the table. "Well, it's—they need to come up with a better plan, one that doesn't require a woman to give up her child."

❖

Lee Hyun-eun didn't come to the childcare class the following Wednesday. Neither did she attend the next week. And she wasn't at five A.M. services.

"I spoke with her by the laundry rocks," a woman in the class said when I inquired.

For three days, I crouched behind a distant boulder, keeping my eyes on the spot in the river where women scrubbed their family's clothes against large rocks. No sign of Lee Hyun-eun. When Monday came, I asked Martha to teach my class while I spoke with someone in crisis. Instead I watched the river again.

This time my persistence was rewarded. Before Lee Hyun-eun even had a chance to remove the clothes from the bundle on her back, I was by her side.

"I'm so glad I found you," I said, taking her by the arm, leading her away from the other women.

Startled, she pulled back.

"You must not do it," I said.

"Do what?"

"You must not let them keep him. You must find the courage to say no to the family council."

Lee Hyun-eun looked horror stricken. "Say no?"

"That's right. I'm sure that God wants mother and son to be together. No one can care for him like you do."

She glared at me, her dismay replaced by anger. "Do not speak to me of what your god wants. He killed his own son. Happy all the day? Your god wants mothers to suffer."

Without saying another word, I turned and headed back to the single-women's residence.

❖

In the woods at the edge of the retirement village where we lived, An-hae Pak and I paused every now and then to pick up colorful leaves to decorate the dining tables. Born in Korea, she had come with her husband to the U.S. when they were in their early twenties.

"I often wonder why it is that we talk about many things," she said, "but seldom about your time in Korea. You weren't there long, were you?"

I kicked a mound of golden leaves. "No, just eight months." I didn't want to say more, but she pressed me until I told of my encounter with Lee Hyun-eun.

"And it felt like she rejected you?"

"No—well, maybe. I think I came back early because it—it was humiliating."

"Humiliating?"

"I thought being there would please Lowell. Sort of make amends for him and his buddies having to destroy Korea in order to save it. I was trying to help her. But she got angry."

An-hae stopped and put her arm around my shoulders. "What about now? Now that you're older and wiser?"

"I think—I still think she should have fought to keep her child."

We resumed our stroll.

"Dear friend," An-hae said after a few minutes, "it wasn't just about a woman having to give up her son." She paused to pick up a large red maple leaf. "In our tradition, the spirits of the dead stay around for three generations. It's the oldest son's responsibility to care for the grave and ancestor tablet. If a man has no son, who will care for these things when he is gone? Who will keep the memory alive?"

"But the whole idea is built around superstition."

An-hae peered at me over the top of her bifocals. "Is it? You know what I think?"

"What?"

"I think you need to go back to Seoul."

"Whatever for?"

"In her eighties, a woman has a different heart."

I stand alone on the precipice overlooking Saemunan Street, gazing down at bulldozers clearing away the only remaining traditional building in the block. I'm glad to be free of Rev. Kwan, my doting guide who seems to consider age a malady. I'll get along fine while he attends to other responsibilities.

Automobiles have replaced bicycles that used to clog the street, and where the intimate international bookstore once stood there's a giant structure of glass and steel. As I walk back down the hill, I pass embassies and apartment buildings, recalling the shanty town that occupied the land until one day the Seoul government, without warning, razed it.

Stylishly clad women in heels and men in neatly pressed black suits pass by, making me self-conscious of the beige walking shoes I'm wearing and the pale blue pants suit I found on sale at JCPenny's.

I'm pleased that poverty no longer shrouds the city, but what has replaced it? Thirty-story buildings where residents live in anonymity. Turning the corner I walk by a high-rise apartment building where the mission's single-women's residence used to be. Through the kitchen window of the past I see how young and naïve I was back then—we all were.

Weary, I'm searching both sides of the street for a tea shop when I nearly bump into an iron fence surrounding the frail trunk of a once-proud tree. A sign in Korean and English designates it a National Treasure. How unusual, I think, that instead of chopping down an old tree blocking the way, the city built the sidewalk around it.

Across the street from the tree I enter a tea shop that has modern furnishings and a glass case full of European pastries. Remembering little Korean, I consult my phrase book. "Nok cha, ju se o."

As I sip green tea, I gaze out the window at the National Treasure. It is a decrepit tree, stakes and wires supporting limbs that would otherwise fall off and deprive the tree of its essence. I consider the generations of lovers who met beside it, children who played in its shade. Though it can no longer stand on its own, someone tends it, keeping the memory of the sturdier tree alive.

I feel overcome by an intense sadness. When I die no one will make sure my grave is kept clean or bring my favorite foods for me to enjoy in the afterlife.

There will be no one to keep my memory alive for three generations.

1983
Amy Nolan

In 1983 I grew from 4'11" to 5'3" and from ninety-two pounds to one hundred ten. I was no longer being mistaken for a boy, which had secretly pleased me. I tried to embrace this new phase of my existence—and to transcend it by becoming a woman of shaved down, simple lines and clean body parts—unbreakable, impenetrable, androgynous, and untouchable. I explored the possibilities of this new body in the water, and that summer I began teaching little kids to swim.

Pine Knoll was owned by the military. Its scrubby, sandy property ran up against the National Guard Camp. On a hot day, the swimming pool gleamed like an oasis. It was only five feet deep, but it was wide and long, with a blue water slide that hissed like a fountain.

Lifesaving lessons started at 8:00 in the morning, when there was still a chill in the Midwest air. Groggy but determined, talking gave way to the relentless splash of swimmers as we warmed up with laps. The junior lifesavers were all about the same age: thirteen.

We would teach until four then goof around in the pool as the day became hotter. Sometimes, still in my wet suit, I would bike down to the river after work to wash off the heat, chlorine, and sweat. I'd anchor my feet into the soft sandy bottom, close my eyes, and fall into the rushing current. The breathtaking cold cleaned me from the inside out.

Swimming lessons were run by 4-H, and the instructor's name was Miss Jean. Less than five feet tall, she was perfectly round, had a leathery tan, and long, yellow fingernails from chain-smoking Virginia Slims. In Buddy Holly style glasses, it was hard to tell her age, but she was the one who taught us all to swim when we were in elementary school. Without a pool in those years, she had to take us out in a boat on Lake Margarethe, which was full of weeds and swimmer's itch. There we had to jump in with our clothes on and tread water for twenty minutes before our lessons could begin.

Since we never had a swim team at school, much less a pool, Miss Jean was the closest thing to a swim coach that we knew. She had lived in Hawaii, where she had been a competitive swimmer, although we rarely saw her swim. Her late husband had been in the military. Her hair was always damp and looked like it had been bleached with peroxide.

She barked her commands with a loud, raspy voice as she paced the sides of the pool: "Spaghetti legs! Straighten your legs! Head up! Faster! Don't swallow the pool!"

Although the boys respected her, they made fun of her appearance behind her back, referring to her as a toad or a troll. On the few occasions that she removed her baggy cover-up and dove into the water to demonstrate the proper form for a stroke, we would all stand at the edge of the pool, the girls in silence, the boys snickering. But Miss Jean was never distracted, and she never made a splash. She was all grace.

Miss Jean, the pool, friends, and sunshine define 1983. But even more importantly, this was the year I discovered music videos. Music videos made anything seem possible. Punk and disco had given way to the creative variety of new wave. Everything felt fresh, sharp, and shiny, but there was surrender inherent in the experience of watching, and I developed a new longing — to absorb the fluid image.

Every Sunday after church I'd flop on my bed, stomach growling at the scent of a beef roast in the oven, and listen to Casey Kasem's *American Top 40*. Even the classic rock station had started playing new wave bands: A Flock of Seagulls, English Beat, Human League, and Kajagoogoo.

I was drawn to the British, post-punk androgyny that dominated videos in the early 80s—to men and women wearing eyeliner, dramatic streaks of red across their cheekbones, multicolored hair that took flight. This wasn't just performance, it was reinvention. They were like exotic birds, beautiful with fluid sexuality. They soared and twisted. They hammered out the beats of Eros: joy, freedom, expansion, and emotion.

I spun in circles, arms outstretched, wearing one of my stepdad's T-shirts. It hung mid-thigh, like a mini skirt, as the newly found beat rippled through my body.

Whenever I went to a friend's house to spend the night, I was thrilled if they had cable television. We couldn't wait to experience *Friday Night Videos* or *Night Traxx*, a show that ran on the weekends on TBS. From 11:00 P.M. to 4:00 A.M., we could watch, listen to the music, talk, eat, and critique.

The videos I liked told stories. They were dreams—surreal, mesmerizing, and fragmented with seemingly endless possibilities. I loved the tongue-in-cheek plots of ZZ Top, like "Legs" and "Sharp Dressed Man," in which the band's candy-apple red car carried a trio of sirens who would come to the rescue of put-upon, hard-working people. Their lives, in a matter of minutes, would be graced with a slick, indifferent beauty that seemed desirable after the band graced their harried hero with a talisman, the magic key to good times, a "Z" keychain. Then the sirens would transform him or her into a bedazzled, red-carpet-worthy icon.

I tolerated videos that were really just concert footage; videos of artists from the seventies who were trying to get on the new wave train; videos of male swagger, artists in tight jeans, leaning against brick walls or barns, looking like clones of greasers from the fifties. But then one night, around 3:34 A.M., the Talking Heads' video for "Burning Down the House" came on. Eerie, beautiful, with an energetic drum track, as the music faded a projected image of David Byrne's frozen face traveled along the surface of a dark, lonely road. I was swept away. This was unlike anything I had ever heard or seen — a new portal, not unlike the theater screen, but different, as its smallness seemed specifically created for me alone. It captured the spirit of infinite possibility without resorting to images of sexuality and unattainable physical beauty.

I would sit in the basement, lights out, with my head between the stereo speakers, and let my head and body fill with rich sounds. I'd conjure visions of a world with clear, blue water, ancient ruins, vast deserts, dark labyrinths, and rivers winding through jungles. This gave way to dreams of adventure in worlds that defied comprehension. They pulled at the chest, the head, and that place that was beginning to pull me like a dowsing rod, down to the hum and roll between my hips.

At middle school dances, clammy hands held my waist while mine rested on the shoulders of boys I barely knew. Their eyes, if they would let me see, all had that new look in them. They weren't seeing a friend, someone they'd built a fort with the summer before, or chosen for kickball. They were seeing us as alien to each other. "Footloose," "1999," "Fascination," the virile exuberance of Van Halen's "Jump," all pointed to a future that everyone wanted but could not know until it had been experienced. What we did know, however, from almost every video, magazine, and movie was that this future was inextricably linked to how we looked.

Later that summer, my mother put me on a Greyhound to visit my cousins who lived downstate. She was still trying to shelter my brothers and me from what I already knew: my stepdad's drinking was out of control. Besides going to camp, it was my first solo venture and would take me to the coveted suburbs. Their neighborhood was full of thick, sod-grass lawns, swimming pools, and houses two or three times the size of ours. Everything there was more crowded, somehow more urgent. There were no woods, no rivers to escape to. My cousins and I spent most of our time in a neighbor's pool, where we listened to music, lying in the sun drinking Diet Coke or Crystal Light.

While swimming, I watched my shadow beneath the surface of the pool, where rays of light flew down, casting movement on the bottom. Under water, my slender shadow practiced a wild gymnastics, and I could taste Diet Coke in the back of my throat.

We went to the mall—a multilayered maze of stores full of teenagers, colorful clothes, water fountains, the clean smells of new clothes dye, chlorine, and deep-fried Chinese food. At night, while my cousin slept next to me, I perched on my knees so that I could look out the window into the house next door, where the MTV channel played endlessly. I kept watch all night through the blinds, hoping to catch a glimpse of Duran Duran.

A week later, I was on the bus heading back up north, my mind was a swirling collage of images, feelings, tastes, and smells that I couldn't explain or share with anyone. Something had happened, I had been transformed in some way, but I couldn't express it—I could only feel it. On my headphones radio, Journey's "Faithfully" saturated the heavy, late-summer air. The song's earnest sadness perfectly captured the sense of desolation, road-weary loneliness, and inexpressible longing that I felt in my chest—an overwhelming feeling that nothing was going to be okay, that life from here on out would be replete with moments like these, where language would fail to help me understand my own mixed up joy and grief.

In 1983 I fell under the spell of these shiny surfaces, as I longed to live in a big house like in a John Hughes film, with a perfect lawn and a swimming pool, and be immersed in the suburban world, which seemed so alive and new. By comparison, where I came from seemed isolated, shabby, small—of no consequence, despite the silent natural magic that surrounded me. The trees that sheltered me when I flung myself onto the ground, the river that swept me away when I wanted full immersion, the winding bike trails behind our neighborhood—that summer, in my infatuation with the surface, I would have traded it all in for the gleaming world "downstate."

That summer I went to see Ray Harryhausen's stop-motion film, *The Clash of the Titans,* in the run-down Rialto theatre. My friend Angie and I had snuck hidden cans of Pepsi into the theater, and sat in the front row. Our feet stuck to the floor, gooey from all the years of discarded gum and spilled pop. I loved the dark, cool space of the theater—but most of all, the way I could completely get lost in the massive film screen, which I saw as a portal into wondrous worlds that carried me far, far away—from my family, from the outside world, from nature that seemed only to herald death.

The film is a grand display of Greek myths—specifically, the journey of Perseus. I loved the underwater world of Poseidon, Athena's wise counsel, and the ease with which Pegasus takes wing, but what struck me the most was the sequence in which Perseus must kill Medusa. My palms sweated as I anticipated her impending appearance. Along with horror stories, the mythology of Medusa captivated me. I had never known of a woman who openly expressed so much rage and a murderous desire for bloodshed. I was fascinated by her transformation from beautiful goddess to a scaly monster that turned men to stone.

In the film, Medusa's lair is a labyrinthine, pillared palace gone to ruin. A cloud of loneliness and death hangs over the place, and as Perseus enters the lair, we catch only glimpses of a fake-looking, green, snakelike tail slipping around the corners. As Perseus mounts the steps, the camera's point of view shifts to make his perspective ours. He is handsome, dark-haired, with a cleft chin, and a little sweaty. He brandishes a sword and a mirrored shield. We know that Medusa is watching him; we hear the rattling and hissing that must be her hair of snakes. I know that "Medusa" is fake, but as with all horror films, I put my hands over my face and make cracks of light with my fingers so that I could see if I choose. My friend flipped out and tried to pull my hands away, giggling, "C'mon, open your eyes! Open your eyes! This is the best part! This is where he kills Medusa!"

"Can't I just keep them open halfway?" I pleaded. As Angie erupted into full-blown laughter, I opened my eyes as Perseus' fierce young face filled the screen. To hold myself steady, I looked down at my shoes and tapped them on the gum-infested floor. *I'm still here, I'm still here.* Angie jabbed me, whispering, "Look!" and I looked up just in time to see the back of Medusa's writhing head as she stiffly pulls back her bow and arrow. In one swift moment, Perseus' sword swings, cleanly lopping off the goddess/monster's head. I watched it roll down the steps and into Perseus' thickly woven sack, without his even looking at it. As Medusa's body topples over, fake, too-thick orange blood pours out of the gaping hole where her head had been. I was rapt, struck by how much Medusa's headless body resembled a big, scaly vase that had tipped over, condemned to keep on spilling out its contents, condemned to defeat.

As we leave the theater, as what always happens when I go to movies, part of me is still in the film, and I feel myself emulating the gestures of some of the actors. Medusa's death haunts me. I know that Perseus has to succeed because he is the hero. Everything depends on him and his ability to kill. His worth is determined by this ability. I am relieved that he succeeds, because this is the way it has always been. When the hero predictably wins as the myth dictates, there is a sense of order that we barely perceive. Heroism becomes equal to violence. I would learn later that this was not only living mythology, but it exists within my country's story, and certainly the story of Grayling, Michigan, with its emphasis on military might and male conquests on the football field and during deer hunting season. There is reassurance that there is order in the universe — that good can and will triumph over evil and/or nature.

At the time I saw *Clash of the Titans*, Stephen King had become wildly popular, and his novels were starting to become films. That summer, I had devoured three of his books: *The Shining, Carrie,* and *Christine.* Aside from *The Shining,* in which a frightening female character makes a brief appearance, the latter two novels featured angry, vengeful women — one a high school girl and the other a red '57 Chevy — with whom the reader is compelled to identify. Both Carrie and Christine are transformed from apparently innocent, shrinking violets into formidable, magnificent bodies of horror. Their power is terrifying and beautiful: Carrie, with the gift and curse of telekinesis, literally destroys her merciless tormentors at the prom; and Christine, whose spirit is that of a spurned lover, destroys and terrorizes anyone who comes between her and whatever man takes care of her. To my own adolescent mind, the idea of women being monsters, violent, or predatory in any way was frightening and fascinating. I already knew that men and some boys could be these things. I already knew that women and girls didn't talk about such things, and I would sometimes look away.

I thought again of Medusa, whose visage I had begun to research at the Crawford County Library after seeing *Clash of the Titans*. If I could have asked research questions then, I might have asked, what about the monster? I thought about the lovable monsters on *Sesame Street*, especially the anxiety-ridden Grover. Monsters evoke an animality and soulfulness that I see in everything around me: my stuffed animals that come to life when I give them voices, the ant family under the flat stone in the front yard, the snakes on the river trail, the bees hovering lazily above the raspberry canes. I wondered, even then, just a little, what if Medusa had won or escaped Perseus' sword? What if she goes on in the myth, engendering a wild blend of fear and respect? Was she really as evil as everyone said, or was she just misunderstood? If we could talk to Medusa, what stories would she tell?

In 1983, I was in between. I didn't want to grow up, and yet all of us tried to act older than we were. Sometimes I felt at once like Medusa, fierce and monstrous on the inside, and Dorothy from *The Wizard of Oz*, soft, polite, open, naïve. For me, the scariest and most wondrous part of that film was not flying monkeys or the Wicked Witch but the tornado at the beginning. The tornado is black, wholly convincing in its aliveness. It swirls beautifully, angrily, inevitably—an angel of death on the furthest reaches of the Midwestern horizon.

When Dorothy hits her head and passes out, the tornado lifts her out of a world that doesn't understand her, and she becomes heroic. For a long time I considered her the bravest character in film. Most of all, I loved the sequence in which she becomes "one" with the tornado, spinning toward the unknown.

In 1983, I too wanted to be swept away by something greater than myself, to be eroded and shaped as wind and water transform the world.

SELF-WORTH

The Circle Compass
Marilyn Zelke-Windau

When you love,
you come to see layers —
layers of childhood,
of cardboard box car pulling,
of pebble and sand chewing,
of bat and ball and chalk
and potato races
and manhole cover exploration
and dress up clothes
and sleep-overs.

When you love,
the layers pile on
one atop the other
experiences with friends,
with schools,
with elders,
with lessons,
with life.

The person across the world
becomes the person across the street.
The family from afar
becomes the family downstairs.
You reach your arms out to the globe,
the roundness of love,
the circle compass of humanity.

When you love,
all is possible
and all is everyone,
even those you haven't yet met,
but know, just the same.

The Slope
Theo Greenblatt

Shelley glanced in the hall mirror and flashed herself an unconvincing smile, then swept into the kitchen.

"Don will be home before me," she said to the sitter, whose face fell at the news. "Just tell him dinner's in the oven, and that I'm going straight to my yoga class when I get done with my errands. The kids should get some fresh air — maybe you can take them to the park for awhile?" She scooped up Michael, who was playing with a pile of saucepans on the floor, kissed him roughly, and handed him to the teenager. "And no ice cream before dinner, right? See you later!"

She didn't wait for a reply, knowing that Michael would scream if she prolonged the act of separation. She shut the front door behind her and trotted down the brick walk to the gold-toned minivan parked in the driveway. Exhaling forcefully, she slid into her seat, turned the key in the ignition, and slid in a CD. Aretha Franklin burst forth from the tiny speakers.

"R-E-S-P-E-C-T, Find out what it means to *me*!" Shelley sang along at the top of her voice, with all the soul she could muster. She swung the van around the curve of the cul-de-sac faster than the neighbors would approve and headed for the main road.

Shelley pulled into the parking lot of the Days Inn, angled into a spot facing the street, cut the engine, and checked her watch. She turned the key partway so that the music came back on and settled lower in the seat. Across the street was Rudolfo's, an Italian restaurant frequented for lunch by the staff of Western Mutual, the insurance company where Don worked. After rechecking her watch several times, she saw two familiar-looking men in business suits emerge from the restaurant across the street. Both carried briefcases, and one had a foil-wrapped doggie-dinner in his hand.

"Perfect, just perfect," she said under her breath. She yanked the key, slung her bag over her shoulder, and stepped out of the car. She looked sideways at the men to see if they had noticed her. She recognized one of them as Tom Wright, who shared a secretary with Don; the other one she'd met at the last Christmas party. Careful to keep her back to them, Shelley slammed the door shut, strode purposefully to the motel entrance, and went inside. Out of the corner of her eye, she saw them staring at the glistening van with the license plate that read "MYPEACH" — Don's choice, right down to the vanity plate. There was no mistaking such a vehicle in a town this size. Even if they hadn't seen her getting out of it — and she was pretty sure they had — they would know who was parked in the motel parking lot at two in the afternoon.

"I need a room," she said simply to the clerk at the desk.

"Right," he answered slowly, playing idly with the small metal ring in his eyebrow — the way some people crack their knuckles or twist their wedding rings, Shelley thought. She quickly glanced down at her own rather conspicuous diamond set, and looked back at the clerk. Too late to take it off. "No bags?"

"No, no bags. I travel light," she replied with a wry smile. "And I'm paying cash."

"I need your credit card anyway — security," he said.

He handed her a form to fill out, ran her credit card through the slider, and then palmed the key card across the counter to her.

"Enjoy your stay, *Miss.*" Shelley wondered if the irony was intentional or if she just took it that way. She decided it didn't matter.

From outside the door of Room 212, on the terraced landing, she could see her own van in the parking lot. Tom and the other man were long gone by now. She slid the card, opened the door with a flourish, and tossed her bag into a chair.

The room had about as much character as a bologna sandwich on white bread. One queen-size bed with a sky-blue spread took up most of the center, flanked by a pair of generic veneer bedside tables with matching ceramic-based lamps. These were color coordinated with the large painting of a seacoast that hung over the bed. A bureau topped by a television stood in one corner, a vanity with a yellowed mirror in the other—all the same dull brown, ¼-inch wood veneer, glued onto particle-board. Shelley was glad for its utter lack of style. The bathroom had clean sky-blue towels folded neatly over the chrome racks and miniature liquid soap and shampoo bottles. Her first inclination was to pocket these kid-size items for Taylor, but then she realized she might use them, since she really had come with no bags.

She kicked off her shoes, grabbed the remote, and spread out in the very middle of the bed. She surveyed the available channels, lingering here and there. On some women's talk show, the blonde hostess was helping to demonstrate napkin-folding techniques. If only I could be interested in this, Shelley thought, I could manage everything. She by-passed several day-time dramas, a rerun of *Dukes of Hazzard*, another of *The Fresh Prince of Bel-Air*; she cringed at the gravelly voice of *Judge Judy* and finally came to rest on a Nature Channel special about the mating habits of blue whales. At least the background music was peaceful.

Shelley shut her eyes for a few minutes and then, as if suddenly recalling something vitally important, she leapt off the bed and lunged into the bathroom. She turned the bathtub tap on full blast and emptied the entire contents of the courtesy bottle of bath foam into the stream of hot water. Then she fished around in her oversized purse, the kind mothers of young children usually carry, and instead of the ubiquitous pacifiers and wadded Kleenex, she pulled out a split of champagne, a small box of Godiva chocolates, and a thick novel. She carried them into the bathroom, popped the cork on the champagne and poured half of it into one of the plastic cups by the sink. She placed the cup and the bottle on the side of the tub, along with the chocolates and the book, and peeled off her clothes. Avoiding the full-length mirror on the back of the door, she slowly sank into the steaming cloud of bubbles.

About a hundred pages later, Shelley drained the last sip of champagne, licked the final traces of chocolate from her fingers, and flipped the tub drain open. She dried herself with the rough but clean towel — that she didn't have to wash and fold, she reminded herself — and tossed it into the corner of the bathroom with a defiant shrug. She pulled the heavy drapes across the window, after one last peek at her van, turned off the lights and slid naked between the smooth, cool sheets. Settling again in the very center of the bed, she closed her eyes and slept.

The wall clock in the front hall, the one with their names and wedding date inscribed on its face, was chiming eight o'clock when Shelley walked in. Don was finishing the nightly bathtime ritual with both kids. She passed the kitchen on her way in and saw the dishes and food still on the table, and the baby's mess — an overturned sippy-cup in the middle of a sticky, purple puddle flecked with rice from the casserole. This was clearly left for her, the price of an evening off. She stood in the doorway of the shell pink bathroom for a few moments, watching, before they noticed her. Bathtime was the one parenting activity Don was willing to perform regularly; he took pride in his vigilance of their safety in the tub. Michael was squirming half-heartedly under Don's touch, as he toweled him dry. They both caught sight of her at the same time.

"Mommy!" yelled Michael, echoed by his half-submerged sister, and ran headlong at her. Don looked up, his face blank and stiff.

"How was yoga?" he asked icily, oblivious to the immediate chill he created.

"Fine," she said, scooping up the toddler and holding him tight. She wondered if Don's coldness could be felt on the little boy's bare skin. She carried him to his room and wrestled him gently into his pajamas. Taylor came in still dripping.

"Look, Mommy, I got all the paint off," she said proudly, holding her hands out in front of her.

"Taylor, come get your nightie on," Don called impatiently from the hall, before Shelley had a chance to respond, and Taylor ran back out. They never run like that when I call them, thought Shelley; because they're not scared of me, I guess.

When the kids were finally tucked in, Shelley returned to the kitchen and began to straighten up the mess from dinner. Don came in from the den and stood in the doorway, glowering. She scooped the cold casserole leftovers into a Tupperware container and slid it into the fridge, put the pan into the sink, sponged up the grape puddle on the floor; all before Don opened his mouth to speak. She knew what was coming, had rehearsed it a thousand times at least, but now that the moment was here, she realized she was slightly afraid of Don. That was something she had forgotten to anticipate.

"How long has this been going on?" he asked without preamble.

Shelley continued sponging the counter, but she shot him a what-the-hell-are-you-talking-about look that she hoped was convincing.

"Don't give me that look, Shelley. Frank and Tom saw you today. At the motel."

Shelley closed her eyes and sighed, but did not speak.

"I think I deserve an explanation, at the very least."

Shelley continued sponging in silence. There was a long pause on Don's side while he waited for some kind of response. Shelley suddenly felt the power of silence; usually she was pleading or whining or angry while Don remained stoic and calm. Now she was in control.

"Shelley, what the hell is going on?" Don finally ground out between clenched teeth.

"Nothing is going on, Don," said Shelley simply.

"Then what the hell were you doing at the Days Inn at two in the afternoon?"

"Taking a break."

"Oh for Christ sake, what does that mean?"

Shelley shrugged, wrung out the sponge, and opened the cupboard for the broom.

"So who were you with?"

Shelley started in the corner of the kitchen, sweeping methodically—she had a system for this—while Don stayed planted in the doorway.

" 'Scuse me," she said, as the broom passed over the toes of Don's wingtips. Now that she was in the middle of it, she was enjoying this more than she thought she would, but a tiny part of her felt sorry for Don. She finished her careful routine, scooped up the refuse from the floor, and put the broom away before Don spoke again.

"Now will you talk to me?" he asked with a mixture of anger and petulance.

"I *am* talking to you."

"About the motel." Don pulled out one of the kitchen chairs that Shelley had just carefully lined up at the small table and sat down heavily. Shelley remained standing, poised as if she was on her way to do something else.

"Hmm?"

"Shelley, Frank and Tom both saw you clearly get out of the van and go into the motel, in the middle of the afternoon. Are you going to deny you were there?"

"I'm not denying I was there," she replied quietly.

"Then who the hell were you with?"

"No one."

"That's ridiculous," Don sputtered.

"I know." Shelley smiled.

"Shelley, I'm willing to put up with an awful lot," — since when? thought Shelley — "but you know the one thing I will not stand for is an affair. I can't stand the thought of you touching someone else; it makes me sick. I'm not hanging around for more of this, if that's what's going on."

Shelley realized that this was the pivotal moment, a peak from which one could only descend. What she said and did in this moment would determine whether Don would slide down the slope away from her, or the two of them would tumble together back into the same familiar territory they had shared for the past six years. She felt like she was on a game show with the timer music pinging in the background. Her turn would be up in seconds, she had to say something, the exact right thing, make the perfect move, to swing this the right way. She took a deep, audible breath and slowly brought her hands up to cover her face, rubbing at her eyes and forehead as if the stress of his words was unbearable. She strove for the perfect blend of guilt and contrition in the gesture, while her words remained utterly truthful.

"I've done nothing I feel sorry for, Don," she almost whispered. "You do what you need to do."

Don stood up fast, the flimsy Bentwood chair toppling behind him, and came at her with both hands raised but open, as if to catch a large, heavy ball. He stopped short only inches from her, looking down, his big hands on either side of her face. She could see the veins standing out in his forearms from the strain of holding back. He had never hit her, but he was not above threatening. He lowered his hands to her shoulders and gripped her hard.

"Is this what you *want*, you bitch? You *want* me to go?" Tiny drops of spit flew out of the corners of his mouth as he spoke. Panic welled up in Shelley. She didn't want him to stay out of spite; it would be the worst possible outcome. She had made a deal with herself ahead of time, however, not to say a word that wasn't true in this confrontation. She could see him sliding in the right direction, down the other side; he was just clinging by his fingertips now; and she was willing him to let go. She felt tears welling and stinging in her eyes from the fear that things would go wrong after coming this far, and she suddenly knew what to do. She looked up at him so he could see her eyes fill and brim over; a tear rolled down one cheek. His face changed — she knew his expressions so well — he thought she was sorry, that leaving would hurt her.

"You'll eat this, Shelley. Remember I said so."

Don turned and stalked into the bedroom. Shelley picked up the chair that had fallen and sat down on it, resting her elbows on the table. She heard the closet light go on, the scrape and thud of a suitcase coming down from the highest shelf. Drawers flew open and shut, a belt buckle hit the rim of the suitcase, hangers clanked and rattled. At last, the long, dry screech of the zipper as the case was closed.

Luggage in hand, Don stood for a moment glaring at her from the entranceway. His head snapped to one side and he huffed like an angry horse, then he yanked open the front door and went out, slamming it shut behind him. Shelley pictured his Lexus careening into the parking lot of the Days Inn and appreciated the irony.

Would she "eat this" she wondered? She knew that, as surely as she had pushed Don down one side of the slope, she would slide down the other, leaving behind the house, the car, the charge accounts. When Don found his footing, he would make good on his threat. Shelley shook off this vision of her future, a visible shiver running through her.

Whatever I have to *eat*, it will go down smoother with ice cream, she thought. She pulled a tub of Breyer's Mocha Chip out of the freezer and scooped a gigantic helping into a cereal bowl. Turning off lights as she went, she made her way to the bedroom, slid off her jeans, and settled herself right in the middle of the bed, with all four pillows piled up luxuriously behind and around her. She turned on the television just in time to catch the rhythmic opening music of *NYPD Blue*. Yeah, that *Saved by the Bell* kid is still cute, she thought to herself, and dug her spoon into the ice cream.

The Young Woman's Dive Bar Digest
Katie Anderson

Your girlfriends would tell you to avoid this bar. They'd tell you it's the sort of place where drunks and creeps and losers hang out. They'd say you can't meet anyone *good* in a place like this. And you know you're a good girl with a good education, who has good girlfriends, accepts goodnight kisses, prays to a good God for a good life, and knows that good girls just don't go to places like this. This bar is bad.

It was unusual then, that you should have come here one cold, snowy night in late December, leaving behind the safety of your familiar suburb to slum it in the old working-class neighborhoods of Metro Detroit. Your Spidey-senses tingled; your white-girl intuition fluttered in your gut, told you something was amiss as you pulled your car into the lot behind the bar. You hesitated to move your fingers from where they gripped the keys in the ignition, the car now silent but for the phantom sound of Ke$ha and suburban radio.

Indeed, it was quite out of character for you to fancy exploring this realm of spontaneity, a realm reeking of danger and wild excitement. You didn't really know what to expect, but there was something romantic in this mystery, something undeniably alluring, and that was enough to give you the needed courage to exit your car and approach the bar door, where a thrilling new adventure lay just beyond the threshold.

Well, you realized soon enough that this wasn't some mysterious, exotic place. No ifs, ands, or buts about it; this was just a bar. It was a neon flashing, dart throwing, pool shooting, jukebox humming, dream killing, dirty dive bar. And as the walls of your imagination began to crumble down around you, a most obvious nugget of truth emerged from the rubble: *I'm in a bar. I should get a drink.*

You approached the wooden bar top and took a seat on the nearest stool, closest to the door, up against the wall, and ordered a vodka cranberry. That was your first mistake. Maybe you had no idea what you did was wrong, but when we saw the look on your face, like a pup caught pissing on a rug, something told us you knew better than to order a pink drink in a place like this. Yet it was too late by then, because when you'd met our curious stares we didn't need no pink drink to tell us what you were made of. Giving up all that information, that was your second mistake. And the look in your eyes said you had figured it all out on your own, that good girls don't go to places like this.

You didn't have to think it was true, but you did. That was your third mistake. I almost thought to sit down beside you and order us a round of beers, or whisky, or anything that didn't contain cranberry juice. I thought I could take you under my wing, get you to come across the room with me, and shoot a couple games of pool with the rest of us bar flies. I even thought for a moment when we made brief eye contact that you were thinking you'd accept that silent invitation. But if you really did see me, then you did not dare acknowledge it, so I let you be. And I guess I didn't want to spoil the moment for you anyways, however fraught with silly faults and unspoken blunders, however humiliated and endearing though you looked; I hope someday you'll look back at that experience and wonder why you gave a damn about what those drunks and creeps and losers thought. I hope someday you have a good long laugh over that time you let a vodka cranberry get the best of your nerves.

But for whatever it was worth, you stood your ground for the moment. So I watched, and I waited.

People measure their lives in days and months and years as much as they do in chapters. *Those were the years before the kids were born,* someone might say, or *that was after I left the job at the investment firm.* When Joan Didion once famously wrote, "We tell ourselves stories in order to live," I believe it was these stories she meant to do justice to; we organize our lives by these events of change. We keep a table of contents to mark these memories for when we lose our direction so we can recall them in times when we feel life has swallowed us whole. We need these stories because they govern the needle on our moral compass, because page by page our stories teach us a little more about who we are as individuals and what we're made of in a social context. We are truly nothing if not walking, breathing, living narratives from the cradle to the grave.

Our lives are thus continuous, never-ending stories, like those perfect novels we can't put down though we dread the thought of them ending. Our lives are actually not terribly unlike our favorite fictions. All great novels operate according to a certain set of principles that allow a plot to progress: the plot *must* move forward. The plot *always* moves forward, and it does so through the introduction of either a physical conflict or an emotional conflict. And more often than not one will coincide with the other. How often have we heard the tale of the person who had a nervous breakdown and decided to skip town and start a new life? How many mothers have been humbled and awed by the way in which having children deeply changed who they are as emotional beings?

Most of the time, we aren't aware of how these stories have changed us until we've looked back at the previous chapter in our lives. Sometimes we aren't even aware that we've changed until someone else points it out for us (what woman hasn't heard from her elders, "when did you become such a young lady?"), or until we're faced with a situation that forces us to question why we're making a certain decision. If one is lucky enough to be born a woman, her feminine intuition might be powerful enough to allow her the ability to pinpoint the exact moment when life delivered her a hard left turn. She might find that she can recall just how it happened and begin to dissect its meaning — to figure out *why* it happened and not just *how*. And sometimes, if she is intuitive enough to catch it, if she's trained her brain to do so, she can catch herself in the moment just before everything's about to change, when she is approaching an intersection and is close enough to read the stop sign, close enough to decide whether or not to turn or keep going, to order another drink or settle up her tab; I *live* for these moments.

Now I'd be lying if I said that I knew change was coming that first night I went to The Tavern. And if a person were to ask me about the precise moment I began to consider myself a regular, I wouldn't have an answer for that either. But for two years I belonged to that Tavern as much as it belonged to me. There was a certain comfort that came with stepping into that bar, stepping into a room of familiar faces that lit up when they saw me, faces that eagerly welcomed me into their company. It's an undeniable truth that people *need* this sort of comfort.

For two years, I lived my dive bar fairy tale, and it was everything I could have imagined. The Tavern was like this secret hole in the wall — dense and dark and teeming with my most ridiculous fantasies. I was going to find out who I was in a place like that, staring down the shaft of a pool cue, drowning in a pint of Budweiser; I was going to punch through that wall and plunge head first, with no regrets, into whatever adventure lay ahead.

And so I did just that, which inevitably shed a little outside light on the circus within. I smoked myself stupid on those musky, tavern fumes; I got high on this new life. But every time I went over there for a drink, the hole got a little bigger, the space got a little brighter, and the smoke slowly dissipated into a haze. For a while I could see just enough to make out my shadow projected on the back wall behind the pool table, a perfect, hourglass silhouette taking her stance over the pool cue. I think about the way I used to gaze upon that miraculous shadow of a woman, imagining the badass future she had ahead of her, what a big deal she'd become if I could just see her more clearly. Looking back, I probably should have left that hole the way it was.

These days, I like to think of myself as something of a dive bar darling. I drink Dewar's and soda, know my way around a pool table, and approach a jukebox the way a priest approaches an altar. There's this new bar I like to go to regularly, but I don't dare call myself a regular like I did in the old days; my motives just don't quite fit that description. And yet, the owner of my new haunt keeps my scotch in stock, all of the bartenders know to serve up my drink with a side-stack of quarters, and I maintain a certain level of respect with the regulars, which I've naively convinced myself has everything to do with my intelligence and nothing to do with my youthful good looks and charming sense of humor.

See, I'm in my mid-twenties, and I'm just not there yet. I won't let myself be there yet. Because I fear that to settle for this comfort would be to openly admit defeat, to forfeit my youth, and I'm just not ready to shelve my dive bar fairy tale.

I surely don't remember when I decided to become a regular at The Tavern, but it just so happens that I remember the hard left turn I took in deciding that I'd never go back. Because the wall *did* come down, the bright blinding truth burnt up the dive bar darkness, and my lungs cracked with each sober breath of air I drew.

It happened on a Thursday night while I was shooting pool, as I most often did on any night of the week. I remember thinking to myself, *if I've finally become the woman I've always wanted to be then why am I not happy?* Well, it took me a while to figure that one out, but a couple of years later, after closing that chapter in my life, I'd finally come to a sound (though slightly pathetic) conclusion: I may have been able to see clearly what that dive bar was, but it would never see me for who I am. That's the problem with belonging to a dive bar. They never satisfy, they only tease.

So I thought to watch over you that night. I thought I could tell you the truth about this place, about your life. I watched you shift uncomfortably in your seat, then remove your scarf and jacket, sip your cocktail through a pair of rosy, chapped lips. You shook off the snowflakes that peppered your lovely, straight, dark hair, and all the men watched you, waiting, wondering about you. You could see them through your long lashes, in your peripherals, through the wisps of hair that hung willowlike around your face. They caught you looking at them like that. It made them thirsty; it just made you nervous.

You pulled your cell phone out of your pocket and checked for missed calls, for text messages, voicemails. You even checked your Facebook and Twitter and email, anything to make yourself look occupied and unapproachable. You continued to sulk in your cocktail, awkwardly check your phone every couple of minutes, and pointedly frown at anyone lucky enough to catch a look at your pretty, young face. You wondered what the hell you were doing here, caught in this nightmare, surrounded by drunks and creeps and losers, by men who stripped you naked with their eyes and women who looked like they wanted to tear your hair out at the roots. You cursed yourself for thinking you had any business being in a place like this.

And I watched you make a painful decision right then and there, when you slugged back what was left of that pink drink, when the bartender asked if you'd like another one. I watched your moral dilemma from where I stood across the room, shooting pool like I most often do on any night of the week. I watched you look into the bartender's face, and I could have cried for you. Because I was you once, sat where you're sitting now, know exactly what it was you came in here looking for, here in a place like this. You, young, twenty-one or twenty-two, wanting more from your youth beyond the uninspiring boys that belong to your "scene," beyond beer pong and hall crawls, frat parties and Friday Night Lights, beyond the trivial bullshit that makes up twenty-first century, twenty-something social culture. You, constantly searching, hunting for something else, needing release from it all, could you maybe find what you're looking for in a place like this? I watched you think it through; I watched all of this.

And when you paid your tab and left, I watched that too.

End and Beginning
Thelma Zirkelbach

I stand in the vegetable aisle at the grocery store, my hand frozen in the act of reaching for a can of green beans. It's 1965, and here I am, in my teased Sixties hairdo and my cotton shirtwaist dress, facing a crisis that's Not. Supposed. To Happen. Not to me, commemorated in my high school yearbook as a "dear little, neat little, sweet little girl."

I've achieved the goal of every young girl growing up in the Nineteen Fifties. I'm married with two children, a nice home in Houston, Texas, two cars, one dog. I belong to the League of Women Voters, am an officer in my chapter of the Women's Zionist Organization, and faithfully carpool my children to preschool and playdates. Yes, I am June Cleaver personified (minus the pearls). Each afternoon finds me in the kitchen, clad in frilly apron, fixing a delicious dinner for my version of Ward Cleaver. Except that Ward has quit coming home for dinner. He's been "working late," slouching in at 2:00 A.M., heavy-eyed and smelling of sex. The children, who are still in preschool, haven't noticed anything amiss. Their father, a pharmacist, works until ten every other week and comes home after they are asleep. But surely he realizes that I notice we're no longer having our late night snack and talking about our day. Instead, I am going to bed snackless and crying myself to sleep. Would Ward treat June this way? I can't imagine Ward Cleaver having an affair and if he did, he wouldn't be so blatant about it.

Still, I cannot give up the dream, even though it's become a nightmare. What would my family think? What would the neighbors think? One of my mother's favorite sayings is, "Never air your dirty linens in public," and wouldn't getting a divorce be doing that?

What would the other carpool moms whisper about me? Not only would the divorce stigmatize me, but I'd probably have to get a job. Recently one of the carpool families moved away and I suggested we replace her with a new neighbor whose children would be attending the same preschool. "Not *her*," someone gasped. "She *works*."

I grab a can of green beans, drop it into my cart, put it back, eye the peas, and finally select mixed vegetables so I won't have to make a definitive choice. I'm disgusted with myself. If choosing vegetables is so difficult, how can I decide what to do about my marriage? But isn't not deciding a decision in itself?

I drive home, return to my marriage, resume the façade, keep my secret. But the stress of living a lie takes its toll in weight loss, colds, migraines. At the doctor's office, I burst into tears during a relatively painless treatment. My relationship, if one can call it that, with my husband becomes distant, angry, and almost meaningless. I feel out of control.

I see a counselor, and for one hour a week, as I pour out my pain and anger, the tension dissipates, but at home it returns.

On the way to a movie, my spouse and I have an altercation, shouting at one another in the car. When he parks, I jump out, stumble into a phone booth and call my counselor. He advises me to take a cab home. I do and find the babysitter gone and my husband sound asleep. He hadn't even bothered coming after me. How much longer can this continue?

I dream of packing up the children and running away. I'll go out west somewhere, maybe Salt Lake City, find a little apartment, get a job in a bookstore. But of course, I won't. One day when my husband and I are in the backyard, I fantasize grabbing a shovel and bashing his head. Horrified at the violent image, shocked that I imagined such an act, I quickly bury the thought.

On impulse, I hire a private detective to follow him. There's something perversely exciting about this. I've left family entertainment behind for a part in a B movie. The detective reports that my husband is seeing a woman from work. I envision his lover, probably a bleached blonde, heavy smoker, slightly older, experienced. The sordid picture makes me ill.

I begin to think more seriously of ending the marriage. I worry how I'll manage. What if the car breaks down? What if the power goes out? I research careers, interview professional women to learn what their lives are like. I tell my counselor I'll have to learn to "think like a man."

I confront my husband. I'm not sure why he agrees to spend the evenings at home. Maybe he's bored with his lover. Maybe she's tired of him. So here we are again in our cheery breakfast room, but across the table, we glare at one another. Finally, on a chilly fall evening, things come to a head. My bridge group is meeting at our house. He says he's going out. "No," I shriek. "You said you weren't doing that anymore."

"You expect me to stay home while you and your friends play bridge? What is this, a jail?"

Perhaps it is…for both of us. "Stay, or get out," I shout.

He gets out. He packs his clothes, tosses his suitcase in his car, slams the door, and roars off into the night.

I call a member of my bridge group and say I'm sick and have to cancel the evening, then I stumble into the living room, trembling with rage and shock. I know my husband won't come back, know I don't want him to. The marriage is over. The next morning, I send the children off to preschool. I'll find a way to tell them later their father has left. In a symbolic act of freedom, I turn off the air conditioner that my husband insists on running until mid-winter and open all the windows. Then I put on make-up and go to a meeting of the League of Women Voters. I refuse to let my husband, or whatever his title is now, interrupt my daily routine. The following day I take the car to the dealership to investigate a rattle in the engine. "Hah," I exult. "I managed on my own. That was easy."

Divorce is not so easy. The following summer I try to register my children for day camp a few days past the deadline. I explain that I'm newly divorced and attending a master's program so I can return to my career as a speech pathologist. The director's lip curls. He stares at me as if I'm an insect invading his pristine office. "I might make an exception if you were a widow," he says, "but a divorcee—it's not possible." He says "divorcee" as if it's a disease.

My insurance agent says my rate will go up. "Divorced women are prone to accidents." I pay the extra but vow that next year this man will be my ex-insurance agent.

Nevertheless, I find divorce less problematic than a miserable marriage. My parents agree to support me and the children until I finish my master's degree. The women's movement has taken off, and I'm excited to be a pioneer of sorts, no longer "just a housewife" but a student, learning new things and contemplating a career. I enjoy being solely responsible for my children. They have story time and charade time and indoor picnics on rainy days. And finally I decide it's time to venture out into the dating scene.

As nervous as I was in junior high, I attend a singles' gathering. When one of the men hears my last name, he asks if I know a friend of his from college, and names my ex-husband. "I know him," I answer breezily. "We have children together." This does not go over well. The man wanders away.

I decide if I'm going to date, I may as well meet someone intelligent. I take the test for Mensa, an organization for people with IQ's in the top two per cent. I pass and join. At my first Mensa party, I scan the room. No one there appears smarter than the people at the other party. I paste on a fake smile and sit on the stairs, wondering how long I should wait before slipping out.

A tall gangly man with blue eyes and a crew cut sits down next to me and introduces himself. We chat briefly, and he moves on to the next woman. The following afternoon my phone rings. "Hi," the voice says, "this is Ralph Zirkelbach." The name doesn't ring a bell. Probably trying to sell something. I'm about to hang up when he adds, "I met you last night. I was wondering if I could come by this evening."

Now I remember. Why not? "Okay."

During the visit, he asks one question after another. "What is this, an interview?" I ask.

He laughs, apologizes, and invites me to a movie the next weekend. I consider. I'm Jewish, he's not. But I do want to date, and he'll be good to practice on. I say yes.

It's February, and he brings me a Valentine with my name misspelled. I think that's rather endearing. We see *The Shoes of the Fisherman* and go out afterward for coffee. We talk and laugh and gaze at one another, and something clicks. This is more than just a date. Two years later we're married.

It's the Nineteen Seventies and my life has taken a new turn: a happy marriage, a career, three children—one his, two mine. No longer June Cleaver, I've morphed into a working mother version of Carol Brady in *The Brady Bunch* with a smidgeon of Mary Tyler Moore thrown in.

And what have I learned? Well, first of all, it's true that you have to kiss a lot of frogs before you find your prince. And second, Ivy

Baker Priest, United States treasurer under Dwight Eisenhower, was right when she said, "The world is round, and the place which may seem like the end may also be only the beginning."

Recession Survivor

Helena C. Eke

I see the writing on the wall, with my brain's eye.
The rumors have been in the grapevine for a while.
The day is here. Again.
The first Wednesday of the month, whispers Jane.
Sitting in our office, I hear the whispers, hushed phone conversations
See the furtive glances, deserted hallways
Hear the familiar dead silence of layoff day.
It's always awkwardly intense, the larger the quieter
A day of mourning for the living.

My manager tiptoes by and whispers to us
"In strict confidence, we are letting go of Suzie.
She was just told this.
She is taking it well and will be escorted
out of the building by Security
We are really sad to lose her especially after all
the great work she has done.
She was a very valued member of the team and will be missed
I wanted to tell you in person. This is a hard time for all of us…"
Blah blah blah and Bull shit!
Who said you had to let her go? We all know you never liked her.
She challenged your thinking.

Who said a company earning billions has to fire thousands at the first mention of recession?
Who said we have to send fathers and mothers, sons and daughters, to the pavements and unemployment centers?
Living beings with school loans unpaid, mortgages, sick dependents waiting on one paycheck?
Yet all casually disposed of, like a used wad of tissue
You terminate an employee whose excellent program was launched company-wide last week
Her ideas and work won so much praise and executive endorsement
And now, you "just don't have the budget"…"She's been here too long"…"Stuck in her ways"…
Blah blah blah and even more Bullshit!

Oh shut up with the excuses.
It's politics. Corporate America at its worst.
It's the rat race, the survival of the cunning and sacrifice of the honest/callow.
This is not for the team, it's for more money, it's for you.
It's not performance-based, it's you retaliating, you bully.
It's not justified, it's you, you speech-swallowing capitalist puppet
It's not necessary, it's Greed. You cut the souls and bring in
more machines.
But remember, you executors of greed's will, "Karma is a bitch"
who sure gets around.

Sticky Notes
Trina Sotira

I put a call out to my friends and family through e-mail to see if anyone would help me move. The response was overwhelming. Cousins and neighbors, friends and children came to load the moving truck. Frozen with fear of what lied ahead, I had no idea what I was doing. All I knew was that I had to go. And all my moving helpers knew was they could not touch the furniture with a yellow sticky note labeled "stays." Only the "goes" furniture would leave the divided house.

The loaded truck pulled away, leaving me alone to capture dust bunnies gathered in places where beds once rested, cleaning the house before my ex returned. I drove myself in my SUV filled with important items like years of unsold manuscripts about talking bears and summer campers—most of them about broken families—and made my way to my new home. I did not have the luxury to feel fear at this point; I had to get everything set up for my boys so they would feel comfortable inside strange walls.

When I pulled up the long driveway beside the moving truck, my late grandmother's lion-face bench was already placed between two round bushes. Inside, my friends put delicate dishes in unfamiliar cabinets, others set up my bedroom, while another friend arranged towels in my bathroom like sculptured art. Family members filled our closets with clothes while one friend reassembled the boys' bunk beds, placing animals around pillows and hanging pictures. After months of the emptiness left by divorce, I felt loved again, like someone actually cared. From that day on, the new rental was a community space where every room was created by a collaborative of love.

We had a good month in that home.

As a single mom of two young boys, I found myself at the mercy of the child-support system, waiting for checks to direct deposit. Years earlier, I was one of a team of news producers and anchors who exposed problems with the disbursement unit—now I was the one hoping checks would arrive on time. But when my ex-husband quit his job after the child support unit took out the first installment of money, funds were sparse. (I considered that maybe my ex was just as broken as I was and lacked the will to keep working, but sympathy didn't pay the bills.) I stretched meals over days and only concerned myself with having food for the boys and payment for the before-school babysitter so I could get to work.

Nicor called asking me why I hadn't paid the gas bill from my ex's house, and I pleaded with them to release me of that home, faxing the divorce decree to show proof that I was not responsible. But the bill was in my name. I owed hundreds between my rented home and my ex's house. Between the gas, electric, cell phone, cable, and internet, I had to choose what we needed most. My parents paid the water bill. I canceled cable and the internet. What was left of the gas and electric bill was still too much to survive on my meager salary, which went toward food and gas to get to work. When I began to reveal the truth about my poverty, a friend loaned me rent money with a note that said, "Strong women stick together." Another friend came over with a ten-pack of mac-n-cheese, toilet paper, and snacks for the kids. After my sister begged me to apply for energy aid, I swallowed all of my pride and headed to the county building on an ice-covered January afternoon.

Walking past women of several different nationalities, speaking various beautiful languages to their young children, shame sunk my gaze to the brown linoleum floor, worried anyone who knew me might witness my lowest point. How would I explain myself — that with a master's degree and teaching job I was no better off financially than a full-time minimum-wage earning teenager! But just like the times when doctors would poke and prod my pregnant belly, or my sons would spin in-utero causing excruciating pain, I told myself this was for my children. They needed warmth during the winter. To my amazement, the clerk appeared to have great respect for me given my status as an adjunct college English instructor. The state paid my gas and electric payments, and much to my dismay, my ex's bill was covered as well.

On the elevator ride out of the county building, I met a woman who looked my age. "You wouldn't guess by looking at me that I needed help from the government," she said. "I'm a nursing student." Her peacoat covered what appeared to be a Gap-type dress. No, I wouldn't have guessed that she needed government aid, but then again, there I was — an exterior middle-class teacher with the worry-stricken interior of a homeless person. I heard her story in the elevator — her husband cheated and left her with two young girls. When her husband decided he was ready to try the marriage again, she refused. In anger, he quit his job, and she was left without child support.

I realized there had to be thousands, maybe hundreds of thousands of women in our situation, left penniless from bitterness. Just because we find the courage to leave a hopeless marriage does not mean we deserve to disintegrate alongside our children. The woman tried to convince me to apply for food stamps, but even the name — food stamps — made me depressed. I couldn't do it. I was educated and employed, and I would figure out a way to feed my family.

I looked back through the ashes of my marriage and realized that the decline began when I enrolled in a graduate program to start a new career. After spending five years as a stay-at-home mom and working part-time as a substitute teacher, I knew my boys would be in school soon enough, and something told me I needed to prepare to re-enter the workforce. When the boys were in bed, my time previously spent with my husband was engulfed in 18th century novels, early American writers, Romantic poets, and my voracious appetite to make it on my own. I wrote my way through weekends, even when my husband threatened to break the computer to gain my attention back. But it was lost. I was lost. *We* were lost.

While researching for an essay on *The Fortunes and Misfortunes of Moll Flanders*, an 18th century creation of Daniel Defoe, I was awestruck by the similarities that women still face today. Hundreds of years ago, women in London had to marry for money to survive. Moll Flanders became a business woman, profiting from her marriages, moving on when husbands failed or died. A woman couldn't make it without a man's money back then. And as my experience shows, we still aren't in a position to "make it" if we choose to leave a broken marriage. Stay-at-home mothers work tirelessly to care for their children, giving up careers and independence for their families. But when forced to survive without even a portion of their husband's income, they (we) are left at the mercy of fathers who hopefully choose to remain employed and employers who recognize the need to take a risk on the woman with a ringless finger and school photos in her wallet.

Returning to school while being a stay-at-home mother saved my family, and as I lift the wound of my past, I begin to label this story as "stays" to remember my great shifts. But the part about divorce's exorcisms will have to move to the mental "goes" pile.

Hot Pants

Pat Feeney

I had no scruples about flouncing around in hot pants. I just wanted the money.

It was 1973 and the winds of the Women's Movement had swept the East and West Coasts. Even sleepy St. Louis felt the subtle breeze of the storm that was to come.

I should have walked out. I should have said no. But when the bar manager of the Chase Hotel tossed me a pair of shorts no longer than a six-inch ruler — my uniform — I lunged for them.

The interview took place in the storage room off the bar. This was not the Chase of historic dimension, nor was it the Chase Park Plaza of contemporary elegance. This version fell between the messy, sometimes smelly teen, far from the beauty of infancy, and far from the grace of adulthood. An old metal desk sat off to one side of the storage room; papers, ledger books, and empty styrofoam cups littered the top. The rest of the room held metal shelves bulging with supplies: cocktail glasses, napkins, cleaning supplies, and hot pants. A musty smell permeated the room. Outside the storage room, the empty lounge bristled with dust motes. The bright lights showed every flaw of the room where I had hoped to work: nicked tables and chairs, stains in the upholstery, greasy carpeting, tablecloths that were a few days past their expiration date. It was mid-afternoon, and there were no customers, so the dimmers were off. The lounge opened for the evening traffic, mostly businessmen jonesing for a good drink. In their inebriated states, they would tip well, I imagined. I thought I could seduce the money from their wallets like a magician levitating knives. I was wrong. But that realization came later.

The manager—I think his name was Lew—looked eerily familiar, like a character actor in the role of skanky bar boss. A plain brown belt spanned the top of his expansive belly, the equator of his global mass: barrel chest, thick neck, doughboy arms and legs. His head rested in the middle of his shoulders, its only distinguishing feature the bald pate and a scattering of hair like a Trappist monk's.

The interview was brief.

"How old er ya?" Lew stood back, shooting me a laser stare, daring me to lie.

"Twenty-one."

"Got proof?"

I produced my driver's license from the back pocket of my jeans. I didn't know how to dress for an interview to be a cocktail "waitress," the term used to describe women who delivered anything to a table. As I reached for my license, Lew stared at me, his eyes in a squint, his head tilted to the right. He took my ID, stared at it, his mouth slightly ajar, and handed it back with an "Hmpf," signaling skepticism, but acceptance.

"Turn around." No explanation, just do it.

"Why?" I asked. Instantly I felt threatened. I didn't want to turn my back on this low-life in a closet.

"Ya know, just turn." Lew demonstrated what he wanted with a twirl of his hand. He wanted me to give him a 360-degree view of my wares. I was relieved. This was not the first time I twirled my stuff, though I'd never done it in a shabby storage room. When I was 15, I modeled for a local department store and was skilled in model-spin. I executed an elegant turn for Lew.

"What size er ya?" Lew moved on to the practicality of suiting me up for the field.

"Five."

"No yer not. Yer a three." Then, the lob of the size three hot pants. "Got boots?"

"Yes."

"Wear 'em. And fishnet stockings. And a fancy white blouse."

"OK. When do I start?" I asked.

"Tomorrow at 7:00. And wear makeup."

"I'm wearing makeup."

"No yer not." End of interview.

That evening I returned to my South St. Louis flat with my size three hot pants. I stared at the textbooks on my twin bed. I had work to do but was too excited about my new job to study. A senior in nursing school, I longed for the day I could work one job. I was excited, thinking I might make enough in tips to drop my work-study job cleaning bloody surgical instruments for Firmin-Desloge Hospital. I mentally ticked off the months — 11 — until I could work as a nurse, the job I thought held the answer to my money angst.

Though I was raised in a middle-class family, I grubbed for money as if a financial apocalypse were on hand. I blame my mother, who was considered progressive in her day. She helpfully told me not to rely on my looks.

"Don't count on good looks. Get an education and make a career. Always have a job."

When she gave me this directive, I was a frightfully insecure 11-year-old living in a sticklike physique with choppy, dirty blonde hair. I assumed my mother wanted to help her homely daughter make a place for herself in the world. I had no way to know I would blossom into an attractive adult. Her advice was a bit confusing, since she had a career *and* was a tiny-waisted-full-breasted-clone of Jayne Mansfield. As she droned on in her characteristic monologue, my mother didn't read the questions in my eyes. She shifted to a contradictory it's-all-about-men stance, as if she feared she damned me to spinsterhood with her earlier direction.

"A man doesn't want to marry a good-looking woman with a hollow head. He'll get bored when her looks fade. A dumb woman without a career has nothing to say."

"At least I'm smart," I said.

"And men don't want to marry a woman who's *too* smart. Besides, who wants to be smarter than her husband?"

I took with me the only piece of the conversation that made sense: always work. Several months later I opened a summer day camp for the neighborhood kids. I walked door-to-door with my hand-stenciled flyers to recruit customers and began my grab for financial security. I fell in love with the sound of quarters slamming against the occasional dollar bill in my shoebox till.

After the interview with Lew, I put together my costume for the Chase. I found a ruffled white blouse and black fishnet hose balled up in the dresser I shared with my roommate; I retrieved my black leather boots from under the bed. I tried on everything; the size three pants were tight, but I figured that was what Lew wanted. Then, I moved to the bathroom and dug through cosmetics samples collected over the years, finding what I hoped Lew would consider "makeup." I smeared a stripe of blue eyeshadow on my lids and outlined my eyes with a heavy black liner. Then I layered on mascara until my lashes felt like thorns. A generous rubbing of blush completed the picture. I knew Lew would expect me to wear lipstick — something gaudy and dark — but I had nothing. Besides, I hated wearing lipstick, so I decided to chance going without it. I stepped back from the bathroom mirror and evaluated my work. I looked slutty, but not "tough." That was the word my mother used for women who looked like they'd been sluts for a very long time. I decided I hit the balance between sensuality and innocence. For some reason, I thought that was the formula for big tips in my new job. Wrong again.

My first night at the Chase, I was surprised to be slinging drinks to a room stuffed with sweaty men in gold chains and polyester leisure suits. I don't know what I expected, but not this.

"Honey, hit this again," a jowly guy called out to me. I could barely hear him. The flashing strobe light kept time with pounding disco music, a din that minimized conversation. I'd already picked up nonverbal bar-speak. A raised wagging glass meant "Another." A hand pantomiming writing meant "Check." An impatient wave of the hand (coupled with narrowed eyes) meant, "I'm one unhappy bastard." This signal could mean the waver got the wrong drink, or he didn't like his drink, or he didn't think I was getting his refills in a timely fashion. I fetched Jowls a bourbon on the rocks and pushed it across the table from a position opposite him. He shot me the dreaded signal: a leering look with a crook of his finger. This meant he had something more to say; I navigated to his side of the table, stooped down, and spoke directly to his reddened face. His belly stretched against the nylon of his shirt. A tuft of wiry hair poked out above the top button.

"You're a cool drink for a parched throat," Jowls slurred.

I acted as if I couldn't hear him over the ambient noise. "Yes, lots of ice, the way you asked." I moved a step back with the smile of a proudly empty-headed but adorable girl.

"Come on, Baby. Don't run off."

"I'll get in trouble if I don't fill my orders," I sighed. "You know how rude some people can be."

"Yeah. Some of these guys can be real assholes." He gave me a lop-sided smile. "You hurry back, OK?"

"OK!" I shot him my best please-tip-big smile and turned to go as he attached his hand to my ass; luckily, I was razor thin, so his thick paw didn't gain traction. Enraged, I was tempted to dump a drink on his comb-over. Instead, I slid away, ignoring the violation. I thought that was the best way to fill the tip coffers. Yet again, wrong.

When I got home that night, I emptied my earnings onto the bed and sorted the change. I had few bills among the coins. When I finished counting, I had less than my usual take at Mr. Steak, an earlier restaurant job where I assumed the wives diluted the tips. I mistakenly thought I would hit the jackpot waiting on their husbands when they were alone. I took solace in the fact that I was new to the job. I simply hadn't mastered the cocktail waitress gig.

Before my next shift, I smeared on a heavier coat of makeup and evaluated my new presentation. Thick robin's egg blue coated my eyelids. In lieu of lipstick, I applied creamy rouge to my mouth, creating a cartoonish effect. I opened another button of my blouse and stuffed toilet paper in my bra. I pulled up a long handful of hair and teased it into a nest on the top of my head, adding another two inches to my height. I noticed my coworkers generally sported big, teased hair and reasoned the men must like it. The new look was a little "harder," as my mother would say, but I thought it would pay dividends in tips.

During my first shift, I could tell some of the staff knew repeat customers who made a point to sit in their stations. I spotted knowing looks and winks exchanged between these men and their waitresses. I knew I could build a client base here. I simply needed to heighten my appeal for the bar set. Sashaying into work with my new look, I was ready to reel in *my* regular customers.

This time I could not have been more wrong in my calculation. As the second evening wore on, I could tell by the weight in my pockets I was making even less than before. I was pissed. No amount of seductive table-waiting made a difference. As I stood at the bar for an order, I surveyed the other waitresses, wondering how I was out-played. Some were nice looking, but I could take any of them in a head-to-head competition. From snippets of conversation on breaks, I knew most of them had worked the Lounge for a long time; in waitressing, this meant they made good tips.

Toward the end of the shift, I had my last break. I slipped out the back door to have a smoke. The January cold whistled through the alley, but I was heated from the job and didn't feel the chill. I lit up, drew my first deep drag, and exhaled before I spotted another waitress leaning against the brick wall. She too, held a cigarette and like me, seemed tired, almost sighing as she exhaled her smoke.

I don't remember her name, but she was one of the waitresses who didn't mind talking. She gave me little hints the first night: tuck extra napkins in your waistband, give a cut of your tips to the bartender for fast refills. Maybe Lew assigned me to her, though I don't recall a formal orientation.

As the two of us stood in the alley, the bright lights that illuminated the exit fell across us. I turned my head and looked at my coworker resting against the wall. I followed the lines that mapped her face. Red lipstick bled into the creases around her mouth. Black roots bordered her brassy, strawlike hair. Deep, dark blotches circled her eyes, visible despite a heavy coat of concealer and eye shadow. This was the first time I saw her in bright light. Though I studied her, *I* felt exposed. I thought I must look ridiculous, the wild clownlike colors screaming from my skin, the face of a child who raided her mother's cosmetic bag.

"How's it going?" She broke the silence.

I took another drag before I answered. I didn't know if I should admit my frustration. I wanted her to like me. I wanted her to see I took her advice. Most of all, I wanted to know how to make more money. I decided she might help me if I told her the truth.

"This place is fucked."

"Yeah?"

"Yeah."

We were silent for a few more drags.

"I'm not making shit. I made more at Mr. Steak, and that's not saying much."

She didn't answer. I thought she might not want to talk. I forged ahead anyway. Once I got started, it felt good to complain about the tightwads who pawed me at their tables.

"How long does it take to get good at this?" I finally asked.

She let out a laugh that sounded like a bark. Then she started coughing. Then back to laughing. When she composed herself, she looked at me with pity in her eyes.

"Honey, that bar" — she crooked her thumb in the direction of the door — "that's not how to make money."

I waited to hear more. She stared at me, as if she were waiting for *me* to say something. Then she jerked her head up and back in the direction of the building. "There. That's where we make our money — upstairs."

I don't know if I understood yet. I was silent. I felt remotely present, as if I digested the words from a loud-speaker at a distant location.

"Upstairs?" she repeated. Though it was a question, it was meant as a statement: If I was too dense to understand, she wasn't going to explain.

I nodded. I understood.

She sighed, stubbed out her cigarette with the toe of her stiletto boot, walked past me to the door, and disappeared into the bar.

I continued to smoke. I lit another, absorbing the dialogue, wondering what my cocktail mentor thought of me. I feared I looked dim-witted, despite my effort to project experience. Oddly, I was fixated on my ignorance far more than the content of the conversation.

I glanced at my wristwatch then stared a long while at the alley dumpster. I wondered if it was too late to stop at restaurants on the way home and put in applications. Then, I realized I was wearing the wrong clothes. I looked down at my long fish-netted legs, the tight hot pants barely visible.

As I crushed the smoke on the brick of the hotel, a shiver crossed my back.

The Last Christmas

Deborah Burch-Lavis

We sat in the makeshift family room on Christmas morning, squeezed into the only corner not covered with stacks of boxes, when it happened.

We had moved into this house six months before but had to renovate over half of it to make it livable. We had not unpacked any of our books or much of anything else yet. We had lived as if camping out. The house was so chaotic that even the cats rebelled, using anything for their bathroom but their litter box. The living room, where we should have celebrated Christmas, was covered in plastic just like the kitchen, the breakfast area, two bedrooms, and a bathroom.

My husband, Sam, and our two children, Sammy and Allison, sat in front of the Christmas tree in this family room. The room, originally a garage, had been converted into an oversized great room, which now held our dining room table and chairs, a china cabinet, bookcases, my piano, a sofa, a recliner, and over 50 boxes. I had managed to carve out a small space for us to sit together with our tree and our presents. We began to open presents as we had every Christmas morning since Sammy was born.

As usual, Sammy and Allison tore into their presents and waited as their dad opened his. I opened mine last as in all past years. I don't remember what Sammy and Allison gave me. All I remember are the gifts from Sam. The first a black quilted North Face vest. I told him how much I liked it and meant it. The second was also a winter vest, a green-gray wool one from REI. I told him I liked it, too, but I said to myself, why two winter vests? It seldom gets cold enough in Houston to wear one, much less two.

Many questions ran through my mind. Did his tendency to wait until Christmas Eve to shop get the best of him and REI was the only place open? Had he completely run out of ideas on what to give me? He always struggled but would fall back on jewelry, which always worked. Or was this his way of telling me that I was cold toward him? I knew the truth in that.

Over the thirty years of our marriage, I had learned to survive by staying a safe distance from him, physically and emotionally. His violent temper and rages terrified me. I never knew what would set him off or what he might do. I lost track of the number of broken objects I had cleaned up, the repairs I had made to the damaged doors and walls, the times I closed my eyes unable otherwise to control my panic when his raging fits led him to speed through traffic, and the bruises I hid from everyone. I had begun to search for a safe place. I could no longer use the kids' schoolwork or activities as buffers. Sammy was off at college, and Allison was attending a boarding school for troubled teens in Vermont.

I found refuge in work. With my new position back in the environment I loved most, the university, I had thrown myself into my work like an alcoholic into booze. I spent most of my time in my office at the university. I stayed late into the evening and came home and worked more as Sam fell asleep in front of the TV.

We only communicated when we had to. Even when young and in love, we rarely talked, and now, we never did. I only called him at work when I knew he was at lunch so that I did not have to talk to him directly. I could just leave voice mail. When he wanted to go somewhere on the weekend, I would tell him I had to work and be relieved when he would go off by himself. We slept together, but the king-size bed allowed me to stay away from him, and my surgery to remove a growth from my breast gave me an excuse to remain at a safe distance. I would recoil if he even touched me accidently while we slept.

So, yes, winter vests were somehow appropriate as a Christmas gift, but it was my next thought I will never forget. It flashed across my mind, and I felt tears coming as it lingered: This is the last Christmas we will have together as a family. And it was.

Two weeks later, we had just sent Allison back to Vermont when I got the call from her. She said, "Mom, if you don't let me come home, I will kill myself."

"Allison, no, no, no. You need to be at the school. It will help you. Coming home is not a good idea. Your dad will never go for it."

"I don't care what Dad says. I'm coming home or else."

She meant it. To kill herself, all she had to do was stop taking her insulin, which she had done before. She had been hospitalized with diabetic ketoacidosis three times in the last few months, and I knew the cold, dark, locked-in winter in Vermont was making her depression worse.

I called Sam to tell him what she had said, and he said, "If you let her come home, I'm leaving."

I hung up the phone, wondering how he could feel that way about his own child. As much as I feared him, this ultimatum was one for which I had only one response. I would let Allison come home.

When I awoke the next morning, Sam was gone. Since he often left home before I woke, I thought he would return at the end of the day, but he didn't. When I got back from the airport late that afternoon with Allison, his car was not in the driveway. Allison asked, "Where's Dad?"

"I don't know. I guess still at work."

I listened all night for him to return home, but he didn't. One day, two, three, a week, and no word.

I did not know where he was. I felt free for the first time in years but also apprehensive. I feared I would wake up and he would be sitting at the end of my bed or I would come home from work and find him waiting in the driveway. Finally, he called and said he was staying in a hotel close by and would be moving in with a friend. He said, "I'll be by shortly to pick up a few things."

I wasn't sure what to expect when he came over, and when he came in, by reflex, I stepped back. He charged in the door like a bull entering a bullring. His size and confidence filled the room as he tore past me through the living room to the end of the table closest to the window in the breakfast room. He stood looking out the window with his back to me. I walked to the other end of the table, close enough to hear him, but far enough away so he couldn't reach me. I stared at his back and waited for him to turn around.

His height and broad shoulders reminded me of a photo of him at 20 when we had only been married two years. In the photo, he stood in parade rest facing the camera dressed in his green army fatigues; he was 200 pounds of solid muscle on a six-foot frame. With black hair and brown eyes and strong features, he was handsome, and his expression told the world he was in command. The thought vanished as Sam turned around and moved toward me. I froze.

He said, "I want to show you how serious I am about this."

This *what* I thought? He stretched out his hand toward me and said, "Here!"

I reached out as he dropped his thin gold wedding band in my hand. I looked at it, noticing the break in it, which had occurred years before and never repaired. I closed my hand around his ring. It felt hot. I looked up at him, not sure what to do or say.

"Okay," was all I could utter.

"I'll call you with the name of a divorce lawyer we both can use."

Again "Okay" was all I could get out.

I tried to think of words to express what I felt, but what I felt escaped words. Then, I watched as he walked past me and out the front door. I closed the door behind him. I felt tears coming but also a weight being lifted from my chest. I took a deep breath. Thirty years — well over half of my life — had passed since we married, and now, he was gone.

I walked through the empty house, passing through the cluttered family room we sat in for our last Christmas together. The boxes were still stacked almost to the ceiling, but the corner where our tree stood was empty. I paused, looking at that corner at a small ray of sunlight shining down through the skylight. A calmness quieted my racing heart for the first time in years. The shadow under which I had lived most of my life was gone. Tomorrow, I thought, I can start unpacking the boxes. Tomorrow a new life begins for all of us.

The New Place

Marianne Taylor

In a house new and empty
no stains in the sink
high ceilinged volume
        deep and echoing

drowning the potted plants
        forgetting photosynthesis, only
curling their leaves, lost
        in the new carpet smell

icy entryway tile pressed against my cheek
        I try to take stock

but these boxes are distracting
and my head hurts from the effort of trying to imagine
a life in this place where the neighbors look so normal
and the children yell like always but your eyes

        turn away
as if to count the bricks in the fireplace and I can't imagine
filling these drawers with cutlery and the minutia
        of a long and happy life

        together
and I see that neither can
you.

It is Not Flesh and Blood, but the Heart
Danita Berg

When we pulled into his driveway, two lanky teenagers, freckled and stringy haired, sat on the porch, peering into the truck at me. I put my hand on my new boyfriend's knee. "Is that them?"

"Yep," he said. "Come say hi."

I bit my lip. Jeff was new; his children, alien. But I'd already fallen for him some weeks before, when he bent me backward over my kitchen island and kissed me until I was lost.

I'd already been lost, a transplant from sun-drenched Florida to windy, dusty Oklahoma, where I'd accepted a job that took me away from the remnants of a failed marriage. In my new state I lived in a vast house that creaked at night, keeping me awake. I'd made the best of icy winters, too-hot summers, and half-awake nights. After two years, I wanted to go home.

I squared my shoulders and stepped out of the truck. The kids smiled at me, kind and distant. They'd been through this routine before with their dad, a serial dater. Buying some time, I fetched everyone glasses of water from the kitchen, eyeing the couch where their father and I had fallen onto each other after our fourth date, his furniture now overwhelmed with his children's laptops, discarded clothes, and other kiddy litter.

Jeff made the introductions. We sat on the porch, me wanting them to like me while I watched their father, wanting him to bend me over my kitchen island again. "You're just a lonely old English teacher," the son accused me, with a 12-year-old's frankness. I grew teary because he was right.

In the next weeks I bought them pizzas for dinner, making excuses to stay late so I wouldn't have to go back to my too-quiet house. We staged horror movies starring the kids in their living room, shooting video on my iPhone, all of us learning to interact. We started to smile at each other with actual warmth.

I met Jeff's family: his parents, his sister, and his ex-wife, with whom he co-parented. They invited me to dinners and birthday parties and included me in the family Thanksgiving photo. Soon my weekends were consumed with domestic activity, the kind I'd craved and asked my ex-husband to give me years before giving up and leaving the marriage.

Within three months I moved in, on a crisp fall day when the Oklahoma weather was almost tolerable. I'd never lived with a man before marriage, not even my ex-husband — he and I hadn't moved in together until months after the ceremony. Jeff carved out some space in his home for me: half of his closet, a child's dresser drawer his daughter loaned me, and a small library room where I kept my books, some couches, and all three of my dogs. I joked that I felt like I was camping with so few of my things there.

Still, I liked being around the silly movies they watched, the noisy exchanges at the dining room table, playing tackle-n-tickle games with them in Jeff's bedroom. At night I listened to the kids breathe in their rooms down the hall, me tucked in with their father, his arm around me. I slept well for the first time in years.

I decided Jeff's kids were on loan. I helped them with homework. I patted their clean clothes when I placed them on their beds to be put away. I helped Jeff wrap their Christmas presents while fighting a case of mono I caught from sharing a Diet Coke with his daughter.

One Saturday I caught the daughter sketching something at the kitchen table. "Whatcha got there?" I asked. She leaned back, exposing a drawing she'd titled "Family," with me smiling and waving a stick-figure hand. I put my hand on her shoulder. When she was finished, I hung the picture on the kitchen wall. I put my old house up for sale, glad to be out of it as the weather grew cooler.

Winter came. My house did not sell. I cursed my new state's severe weather. It was tough to find ways to exercise when I couldn't run or drive to the yoga studio. I started eating the kids' junk food because it was easier. I gained 10 pounds, then 15. The kids got up at ungodly hours to go to school, banging around and talking while I tried to sleep.

"Hey, Danita, you awake?" the son would ask from the hallway in a loud whisper.

"Yes," I lied.

"Last night, when I was playing Skyrim…" he'd ramble about his favorite Xbox game while I nodded and pretended to listen, falling back asleep.

After they left for school, I'd shiver in the house's only bathroom with a shower. I'd pick up their towels, their clothes, hope for some leftover face wash and shampoo. I'd spend the morning cleaning up after everyone since I didn't have to be at work until the afternoon. I used to use my mornings for writing. I tried not to mind.

It became colder. As I drove home from work one night through a snowstorm, I grumbled at my windshield wipers for not moving fast enough. My toes and shoulders hurt from clenching against the cold.

I came home to a dark house and greeted my dogs. "We don't like it here, do we?" I said as they crowded the front door in greeting. "We want to go home." As I herded them to the backdoor to let them in the backyard, I heard giggling. The kids were hiding behind the couch. "You guys are monkeys," I said as they jumped out of their hiding places, dodging my reaching arms as they ran off to their rooms. I loved them more.

Winter bore on, Oklahoma desolate and muddy, then icy. Dishes constantly piled up in the sink. Laundry was thrown into the baskets as quickly as I washed it. The kids' television programs and music got on my nerves. I began to understand what a real mother felt like. I grew jowls.

When my house finally sold, I showed Jeff pictures on real estate web sites of bigger houses, where we could all have some space to breathe, but he was determined to make his house work. I grew to hate the miniscule closet, dresser drawer, and small library room that had no doors, my only respites in the house. I looked at the filthy house and wondered how all of my belongings were doing, stacked into two storage units six blocks away.

Then, I was offered a job with a significant raise in Florida. It was our chance. Jeff's ex-wife dated a man who lived 15 minutes away from the prospective job, and she wanted out of Oklahoma too. We could afford a bigger house that fit all of us. I could have all of my sunshine.

Jeff's face reddened when I told him I wanted to go. His family was in Oklahoma, he said. His parents were getting older. His sister was getting married soon. He had his house, and liked it. He loved me.

"Don't leave us," his son said. "We love you," his daughter said. I looked outside at the ugly park, soggy and grey with no promise of spring. Love emanated from inside the house, but I didn't know how to live outside of it.

I took the job. I showed the kids pictures of bigger houses in Florida, ones where they'd have their own bathrooms and I would have mine. We'd have a pool, I promised. They'd love it. I'd keep right on loving them.

I found Jeff job prospects in Orlando through employment web sites. He would squirm as I filled out the applications for him. I began to feel as though I was an appendage to the family, not a member. I stopped trying.

Eventually, it was time to go. Quietly I packed my things and cleaned the house, stocking it with the supplies I knew they'd run out of not long after I left. I hid from the kids in the bathroom the night before I moved so they couldn't see me cry.

You'll feel better once you get home, my family and friends told me. The kids will forget you. They'll grow up and ignore their real parents soon enough. Jeff and you will find new people to date. Still, I monitored the kids' Facebook pages, watching their lives progress without me in them. Jeff and I made vague promises of them moving here, even though we knew they wouldn't.

My new house was cleaner. I listened to what I wanted on the TV. I started eating better, lost the weight I gained the previous year. I sat with my dogs, equal parts regret and relief, a lonely old English teacher who went home to lose not just her love but also her family.

No Business Card Needed
Michelle Duster

You're a woman about to graduate from college in the '80s. To join the workforce, you are told to wear a blue suit, white shirt, red floppy tie, white stockings, and black sensible pumps. *Do research on the company. Give a firm handshake. Strike up a conversation about something in the person's office. Find common ground. Ask intelligent questions. Laugh at their jokes. Answer questions with concrete examples of past accomplishments that illustrate your "go-getter attitude." Be upbeat and interested. Follow up in a timely fashion with a personal thank you note.*

You are hired.

Be the first one in the office and the last one to leave. Volunteer to do more than your required amount of work. Network. Be resourceful. Join professional groups. Have a good attitude. Show enthusiasm.

Do everything you can to be a team player!

Wear a "power suit" and enjoy "power lunches" and participate in "power meetings" and never ever show fatigue, boredom, stress, annoyance, or anything but total devotion to your job. In return you will be rewarded. You'll get promoted. You'll get a raise. You'll get a bonus. You'll get company perks such as tickets to plays or sporting events, discounts for gym memberships, or tuition reimbursement. In other words...you'll get ahead and lead a life filled with the "finer things in life." After all, you are a "Future Leader of America."

You were preceded by the "super women" from the '60s and '70s who paved the way. They had pressure to "do it all" and make it all seem effortless. They did their best to be the perfect wife, the perfect parent, the perfect daughter, the perfect neighbor, all while juggling being the perfect employee.

You, as an '80s woman, are armed with the same college degree from the same college as the men. Have the same level of skill. Have the same competency and interest, so surely if you "follow the rules" you will ascend to your rightful place. At. The. Top.

Organize meetings. Do more than expected. Make travel arrangements. Smile. Come up with great ideas. Make coffee. Make copies. Attend professional conferences. Order food. Make your boss look good. Join committees. Put together mailings. Stay on top of industry trends.

Downsizing. Right sizing. Merging. Eliminating redundancy. Outsourcing. Advances in technology. One person can now do two jobs. Or someone on the other side of the globe can do your job for one-third the cost.

Keep an upbeat attitude. Increase "productivity" and "efficiency." Make yourself indispensable.

Doesn't matter…Now unemployed.

Readjust. Regroup. Reevaluate. Reassess. Never let on that you're disappointed, disillusioned, and flat-out pissed. Keep your head up. Stay focused. Retrain. Redefine yourself.

Get job in new industry. After your boss quits, do your job and her job for months with a smile on your face—even with lack of sleep and lower-than-fair compensation. Wait for the promotion or a raise you deserve for the excellent job done. Instead…department reorganized. Generous severance offer. Six months of health insurance paid.

Take control of your financial destiny. Learn the difference between mutual funds, bonds, stocks, real estate investments, treasuries, and life insurance policies. Devise a five year plan.

At next job have tax-deferred money taken out of each paycheck. Automatic withdrawal for savings. Start to get on your feet. Feel a sense of relief and the beginnings of being prosperous. Start to build a comfortable life and even splurge on some new furniture.

Be resourceful. Make yourself irreplaceable. Come up with solutions. Help make things more efficient.

Company moving out of state. Lives disrupted. AGAIN? Profit margins rise.

Get advanced degree. "Where do you see yourself in five years," asks the interviewer who is twelve years your junior. Hopefully on a friggin' island living off of residual income, you think. But instead say what you know they want to hear. You have perfected the art of looking the part, acting the part, being a part of this "work hard and you'll get ahead" illusion of the American Dream.

You no longer care what your title is. Could care less if you have an inner cube, outer cube, or office…or if you have a plant or not — which seemed to be a high priority for several ex-coworkers, two jobs ago. All you care about is stabilizing your life and gaining some peace of mind.

Company picnics. Team building exercises. Corporate retreats. Doing great and hitting your stride. Getting close to your financial goal, then…Wow! Another merger. Another reorganization.

Reevaluate! "It's not personal. Just business," runs through your mind as you unpack the box of belongings that used to be at your desk at the job you no longer have.

Downsize the idea that someone else can define you. Outsource your tolerance for pretending to be someone you're not. Merge your ideas of self-acceptance and inner strength. Create your own measurement of success.

Unpack your dreams. *Travel. Take care of yourself. Get involved in organizations that reflect your true passions. Exercise more. Meet interesting people. Write. Live on less. Spend more time with family and friends. And realize, really realize that…*

You. Are. Okay.

After decades of readjusting, regrouping, reinventing, and redefining, *give yourself the title* of Phenomenal Woman. No business card needed.

In My Next Life

Susan Mahan

It's never too late to be what you might have been. —George Elliot

I'll have to learn to be cunning and sly
to speak with forked tongue while I look in your eye
to not care a whit when I hurt someone's feelings;
in school, when I'm called on, I'll stare at the ceilings
to never allow for the caution of doubt
if you slight me a little, I'll call you right out!
to doubt every Thomas or Edward or Jake
to train as a lawyer but act like a snake
I'll bake no more cookies
I'll learn to eat snails
heck, if I like the notion,
I'll swallow some nails!
I'll try out a skydive
I'll swim the big Channel
I'll tango in high heels
I'll ski wrapped in flannel
I'll chug-a-lug beer
learn to burp on demand
I'll swear like a trooper
My life will be grand!
I'll keep track of lovers
by notching my belt
I won't have to exercise
I will be svelte…

Oh, who am I kidding?
I don't want to change
and burping out loud
for me would be strange
but bring on my new life
I'll take a big bite
I'll revel and frolic,
continue to write
I've found my true calling,
my primary home
It comes from the heart
in the form of a poem.

AFTERWORD

We hope that you have enjoyed reading this compilation of poems, short stories, and essays that capture a wide variety of experiences that have led to personal growth. Although we 35 women hail from different age groups, geographic locations, marital status, parenting status, professions, and sexual orientations, we are all women who are doing what we can to be our best and be true to ourselves.

From adolescence to mature adulthood, women's roles can include that of daughter, sister, aunt, student, wife, mother, grandmother, caregiver, neighbor, employee, business owner, volunteer, and leader. We all have our personal journey that includes our unique combination of setbacks, disappointments, accomplishments, triumphs, and joys. But what we have in common is our ability to take a deep breath, dust ourselves off, learn from our experiences, and keep moving onto the next step.

Hopefully you feel inspired by knowing that you're not alone in whatever you might be going through. There are women who have come before you and triumphed. And there will be women who come after you who you can inspire. Together, we form a sisterhood and we need to celebrate our similarities, while learning from our differences.

– Michelle Duster

CONTRIBUTORS

Katie Anderson is a freelance writer who currently lives in Los Angeles, California, although her home often changes. She graduated from Warren Wilson College in Asheville, North Carolina, in May 2012, and obtained her B.F.A. in Creative Writing with a focus in creative non-fiction. During her undergraduate career, Katie contributed essays to student-created anthologies, including *The Working Word* and *Travel Lust*. She is thrilled to share her story with women everywhere who at one point or another have ever struggled with their own identities. She wants you to know that you're not alone.

Danita Berg chairs the English Department at Full Sail University and is the founding director of the Red Earth Low-Residency M.F.A. in Creative Writing program at Oklahoma City University. She is also the founding editor of *Animal: A Beast of a Literary Magazine*. Her work has appeared in *Redivider, Southern Women's Review, Quay: A Journal of the Arts, Black Market Review*, and *The Houston Literary Review*, among others, as well as the non-fiction collections *Press Pause Moments: Essays about Life Transitions* by Women Writers and *Ain't Nobody That Can Sing Like Me: An Oklahoma Writing Anthology*.

Deborah Burch-Lavis holds a B.A. and M.A. from the University of Houston and a Ph.D. in English from Rice University, where she is currently Professor of the Practice of Writing and Communication. She teaches graduate courses in creative non-fiction and writing and research across the disciplines and undergraduate courses in leadership communication. Her book *Leadership Communication* (McGraw-Hill) is in its fourth edition. She has participated in the Iowa Summer Writing Festival since 2007 and attended the Bread Loaf Writers' Conference in 2010. Currently, she is completing a memoir and writing essays on her travels across Europe and the Middle East.

Jessica Caudill writes down words that people sometimes like to read. She lives in Lexington, Kentucky, and writes for *MOUR Magazine* and the blog *MOUR After Hours*. She received her M.F.A. in Writing from Spalding University and her work has appeared in *Inscape Magazine*, *Zygote in My Coffee*, and *The Writing Disorder*. She has received awards and grants from Kentuckiana Metroversity and The Kentucky Foundation for Women.

Hannah Cook Cross is a poet, teacher, editor, blogger, and stylist who lives with her husband and two children in Arizona. She is the founder and editor of *One Trick Pony Review*, an online poetry journal. Her work has recently appeared in *Enhance, Switched-on Gutenberg, Blue Stem,* and *The Literary Hatchet*. She is an alumnus of the creative writing programs at Eastern Kentucky University and the University of Tennessee.

Helena C. Eke is a business services and human resources consultant working to help education, literacy, poverty alleviation, and people empowerment, especially for domestic violence victims, immigrants, and disadvantaged groups. She holds a B.A. in Marketing from the University of Nigeria and earned an M.A. from the University of Illinois, as the 2007/8 recipient of the Maria Pia Gratton International Fellowship. She also serves on the

Literacy Council of Seattle as Board Director of Development and Governance, the Grameen Foundation in its Bankers Without Borders Corps, and supports other causes in the U.S. and Africa.

Patricia Feeney lives in St. Louis, Missouri, where she teaches at the St. Louis Community College. She is a member of the Crooked Tree Writers, which serves as her writing-mommy-and-daddy: challenging her to eliminate the trite and explore the heart of her essays. To relax, Feeney kickboxes (her only movement from a sitting position) and spends time with her friends, her husband, and their two adult children (when they're in town, not online, not asleep, not with friends, and when all the stars align). Another of Feeney's personal essays, "Complicated Footwork," appeared in the 2014 issue of *The Lindonwood Review*.

Brandy French is the only daughter of an opera singer and a Spanish dancer and was born in Chicago at the end of the Second World War. She has been (variously) assistant editor of *Modern Teen Magazine*, a Pink Pussycat topless cocktail waitress (that's another story!), an assistant professor of English at Yale, a published film scholar, a playwright and screenwriter, director of development at Columbia Pictures Television, an award-winning advertising copywriter and creative director, a psychoanalyst in private practice, and a mother. Thirteen of her stories have been accepted for publication by literary journals, and she was nominated for the Kirkwood Prize in Fiction at UCLA.

Stephanie Gates is an educator and writer residing in Chicago, Illinois. She likes to think that her words are her activism. Stephanie enjoys writing thought-provoking commentaries on various issues and is especially passionate about issues of equity. When she's not teaching, writing, or engaged in learning for personal development, Stephanie enjoys spending time with family and friends—especially if there is good food involved! She also likes dancing, reading, and traveling. Stephanie is featured in a number of anthologies.

Elizabeth Gauffreau is full-time faculty at Granite State College in Concord, New Hampshire, where she teaches courses in critical inquiry and portfolio assessment of experiential learning. She also serves as the Director of Individualized Learning. She has previously published fiction in *The Long Story, Soundings East, Ad Hoc Manadnock, Rio Grande Review, Blueline,* and *Slow Trains,* among others, as well as poetry in *The Writing On The Wall, The Larcom Review,* and *Natural Bridge.* Her most recent publication is a short story in *Serving House Journal.* Elizabeth lives in Nottingham, New Hampshire.

Jessica Glover teaches at Oklahoma State University. She earned her M.A. in 2009 from Missouri State University. Currently, she is working on her first book as a Ph.D. candidate. Her latest work has appeared in *American Literary Review, Aesthetica, Magma Poetry, Reed Magazine, Kindred, Weave, Comstock Review,* and *Moon City Review.* She won the 2013 Mississippi Valley National Poetry Contest, the 2013 Rash Awards, the 2013 Hard Times Writing Contest for creative non-fiction, and the 2012 Edwin Markham Prize for poetry. Her work is forthcoming in *EDGE, So to Speak, Spillway, Pinyon, Off Channel,* and *Broad River Review.*

Theo Greenblatt has experienced many "shifts" in her lifetime, making this anthology a fitting venue for her work: from hippy to punk to Israeli kibbutznik; from marriage to single motherhood to the unrealities of online dating; from retail sales and middle-age undergrad to teacher and Doctor of Philosophy in English. She currently teaches composition at the preparatory school for the U.S. Naval Academy in Newport, Rhode Island—a position she finds challenging, rewarding, and at times a little surreal. She has published several short works of both fiction and non-fiction and is working on her second book-length memoir.

Lois Marie Harrod's 13th and 14th poetry collections, *Fragments from the Biography of Nemesis* (Cherry Grove Press) and *How Harlene Mae Longs for Truth* (Dancing Girl Press), appeared in 2013. *The Only Is* won the 2012 Tennessee Chapbook Contest (*Poems & Plays*); *Brief Term*, poems about teaching, was published by Black Buzzard Press (2011). Widely published in print journals and online, she has received six fellowships from Virginia Center for Creative Arts and three from New Jersey Council on the Arts. A Geraldine R. Dodge poet and former high school teacher, she teaches Creative Writing at The College of New Jersey.

Loren Hecht is an award-winning college teacher, published writer, performer, and professional musician. She holds an M.A. in Creative Writing from San Diego State University, a B.A. from the University of Michigan, and she teaches writing composition and critical thinking at Northern Illinois University in Dekalb.

Ronna Magy is a Los Angeles-based writer of memoir, short story, and poetry. She came onto the planet as the colors of World War II were fading from Detroit's skyline and Sputnik orbited the skies. Ronna's recent work appears in *Sinister Wisdom, Trivia: Voices of Feminism, Up, Do: Flash Fiction by Women Writers, Off the Rocks, Where Thy Dark Eye Glances, Southern Women's Review,* and *Lady*

Business: A Celebration of Lesbian Poetry. She is the author of several English as a Second Language textbooks. Ronna received her B.A. from the University of Michigan and her M.S.W. from the University of California.

Susan Mahan has been writing poetry since her husband died in 1997. She is a frequent reader at poetry venues, including the Boston Public Library. She has self-published four chap books, including *Missing Mum* (2005) and *World View* (2009). She joined the editorial staff of *The South Boston Literary Gazette* in 2002. She has been published in a number of anthologies, including *Kiss Me Goodnight, Solace in So Many Words*, and *Living Lessons*. She has been published in several online journals and has been included in poetry exhibits in Boston City Hall for the last three years.

Charlotte Mandel has published eight books of poetry, the most recent, *Life Work*, from David Robert Books (2013). Previous titles include two poem-novellas of feminist biblical revision — *The Life of Mary* and *The Marriages of Jacob*. She is winner of the 2012 New Jersey Poets Prize. She edited *Saturday's Women: Eileen W. Barnes Award Anthology* (1982), based on a contest she founded to publish a first book of poetry by a woman over 40. She has published a series of essays on the role of cinema in the life and work of poet H.D.

mariana mcdonald is a bicultural writer whose work has appeared in numerous publications, including poetry in *Anthology of Southern Poets: Georgia, Southern Women's Review, Sugar Mule*, and *El Boletín Nacional;* and fiction in *UpDo: Flash Fiction by Women Writers* and *So to Speak*. She lives in the greater Atlanta area, where she is active in the writing community and the immigrant rights movement. She is a frequent reader at literary and community events. A public health scientist, she works in the arena of health equity, addressing infectious disease disparities. She became a Fellow of Georgia's Hambidge Arts Center in 2012.

MK Miller has two degrees and limitless curiosity. Her writing has been nominated for a Pushcart Prize, and she has written essays and journalism about a wide array of topics, including the cultural significance of go-go boots and authentic communication tips. Her fiction and non-fiction have appeared most recently in *Slice of Life, Thick Jam, Revolution House, Verdad Magazine, Tawdry Bawdry*, and *Tiny Buddha*.

Rita Moe earned an M.F.A. in Creative Writing from Hamline University. Her poetry has appeared in *Water~Stone, Poet Lore, Slipstream*, and *DIAGRAM*, among other literary journals, and she was a finalist in the 2013 Nimrod Literary Awards Competition. The mother of two grown sons, she lives with her husband in Roseville, Minnesota, where they tend a northern garden.

Carole Ann Moleti is a nurse-midwife in New York City. Her writing ranges from sweet and sentimental to edgy and irreverent and focuses on women's and political issues. Carole's short fiction, essays, review, and commentary have appeared in a variety of anthologies and literary venues, including *This Path, Thanksgiving to Christmas: A Quilt of Holidays, Oasis Journal,* and *Not Your Mother's Book: On Being a Parent,* and *On Being a Woman.* Her Cape Cod romance novel was published in 2014.

Amy Nolan's non-fiction appears in *Solstice: A Magazine of Diverse Voices, The Bellevue Literary Review,* and several other literary journals. She won *Solstice's* 2013 Non-fiction Award, and her memoir, *The Whirlpool*, was a finalist for Autumn House Press' 2013 Memoir Award. Her essays have appeared in publications that include *Midwestern Miscellany, The Examined Life, Critique: Studies in Contemporary Literature, Cultural Critique*, and *The Red Cedar Review*. She holds a Ph.D. in American Literature from Michigan State University and teaches writing at Wartburg College. Amy Nolan lives in Iowa.

Nancy Poling was a late bloomer who was able to commit herself to writing only after her children were grown and she had retired. She is author of *Had Eve Come First and Jonah Been a Woman*, a collection of stories in which male heroes of Hebrew Scripture are women, and *Out of the Pumpkin Shell*, a novel about women's friendship and family secrets. Her interest in Korean culture comes from twice living in Seoul, ROK, where her husband was a visiting scholar. After twenty-five years in the Chicago area, they now make their home in western North Carolina.

Kara Provost has published two chapbooks, *Topless* (Main Street Rag, 2011) and *Nests* (Finishing Line Press, 2006), in addition to six microchapbooks with the Origami Poems project. Her poems have appeared in the *Connecticut Review, Main Street Rag, The Newport Review, Ibbetson Street, The Aurorean*, and other journals, as well as in the Wickford Art Association exhibit catalog, *Poetry and Art; The Loft Anthology: 2012 Poetry Awards;* and *In Praise of Pedagogy: Poetry, Flash Fiction, and Essays on Composing*, edited by David Starkey and Wendy Bishop. Kara teaches at Curry College in Milton, Massachusetts, and leads community creative writing workshops.

Gigi Rosenberg's writing has been published by Seal Press, *The Oregonian, Poets & Writers, Writer's Digest,* and *Parenting.* She's performed at On the Boards in Seattle and been a guest commentator on Oregon Public Radio. She's the author of *The Artist's Guide to Grant Writing* (Watson-Guptill, 2010). In 2014, she was a Jack Straw Writer working on her latest project, *How I Lost My Inheritance: A Mother/Daughter Memoir.* She lives in Portland, Oregon, where she works as a coach to entrepreneurs and artists.

Wendy L. Schmidt is a native of Wisconsin. She has been writing short stories and poetry for the last ten years. The Four C's—cat, chocolate, coffee, and computer—are her chosen writing tools. Pieces have been published in *Brawler, Three Line Poetry, Verse Wisconsin, Twisted Dreams, Barbie Anthology, No Rest for the Wicked, Chicago Literati, Lake City Lights,* and a winning poem in Reedsburg Farm/Art Festival.

Patti Capel Swartz's work has appeared in several literary magazines and academic journals. Her commentaries aired on PRI International on *51%.* She received three Denny Plattner Awards from *Appalachian Heritage* magazine for poetry and memoir. Her poetry and memoir appeared in *Persimmon Tree* magazine and *Canary.* Swartz has written about lesbian, gay, bisexual, transgender, intersex, and queer issues. Her essay about the Harlem Renaissance appeared in *Midwest Quarterly* and *Bloom's Harlem Renaissance.* Swartz collaborated with musician Doug Smith on plays from oral histories. She teaches writing, literature, and theory at Kent State University, East Liverpool Campus, in East Liverpool, Ohio.

Marianne Taylor is a recipient of the Allen Ginsberg Award, the Helen A. Quade Memorial Writer's Award, and an Iowa Woman Poetry Prize. Her manuscript *Salt Water, Iowa* has been a finalist in a half dozen contests. Her poetry appears widely in anthologies and national journals such as *Nimrod International, North American Review, Connecticut Review, Alaska Quarterly,* and *Alehouse.* She also writes and directs plays and teaches creative writing and literature at Kirkwood Community College. She lives in the small town of Mount Vernon, Iowa, with her husband and four sons, where she serves on the city council.

Oubria Tronshaw is mother, wife, lover, daughter, student, sister, friend. She received a B.A. in Creative Writing from Santa Fe University of Art and Design and an M.F.A. in Creative Writing from Chicago State University. She loves to read, talk, listen, ride bikes, daydream out of windows, kiss soft cheeks softly, and sink her hands into kinky curly hair. She has decided to live at least a century, but it will be impossible to tell, because she's also decided to stop aging at 34. She truly appreciates you for reading her work, and she hopes it helped whatever needed helping.

Susan Winstead is a native of Chicago, Illinois, and a veteran of the U.S. Army. She is the 2010 recipient of the Ann Darr Scholarship for Female Veterans and Active Duty Military Personnel, awarded by the Writer's Center in Bethesda, Maryland. Her other writing credits include winning the novel competition at Sand Hills Writer's Conference and the non-fiction category of the Porter Fleming Writing Competition — both in Augusta, Georgia. She has had numerous short articles published. She serves on the board for Off-Campus Writers Workshop and Jane's Stories Press Foundation. She lives and works in suburban Chicago.

Marilyn Zelke-Windau is a Wisconsin poet and a former elementary school art teacher. She enjoys painting with words. Her poems have appeared in many printed and online publications, including *Verse Wisconsin, Stoneboat, Fox Cry Review, Linden Avenue Literary Journal, qarrtsiluni, Your Daily Poem*, and several anthologies. She is a member of the Wisconsin Fellowship of Poets. Her chapbook *Adventures in Paradise* was published by Finishing Line Press (2014).

Thelma Zirkelbach is a multipublished author of poetry, essays, memoir, and romantic suspense. Her most recent publications are a memoir of her husband's last year, entitled *Stumbling Through the Dark*, and an anthology she coedited, entitled *On Our Own: Widowhood for Smarties*. She is a semi-retired speech pathologist who lives in Houston, Texas.

PROJECT EDITORS

Michelle Duster is a writer, speaker, and personal historian. She cowrote the children's history book *Tate and His Historic Dream* (2014). She compiled and edited *Ida In Her Own Words* (2008) and *Ida From Abroad* (2010), which include the original writings of her great-grandmother, Ida B. Wells—journalist, civil rights activist, and suffragist. She was also a contributor to the books *In Spite of the Double Drawbacks: African American Women in History and Culture* (2012) and *Women Building Chicago: 1790-1990* (2001). A native Chicagoan, Michelle earned her B.A. in Psychology from Dartmouth College in Hanover, New Hampshire, and her M.A. in Media Studies from The New School in New York City.

Trina Sotira is full-time English faculty at College of DuPage, where she teaches creative writing and advises the student-juried literary journal, *The Prairie Light Review*. She earned her B.A. in Journalism from Columbia College Chicago and her M.A. in British and American Literature from Northern Illinois University. Trina produced television news in Chicago and Rockford, and most recently wrote novels for teens. The e-release of her young adult novel *In Her Skin* (2012) received recognition for revealing the struggles of a transgender teen. Her flash fiction is featured in *Emerge Literary Journal*. She is raising her family in a town where she can see the Chicago skyline in the distance.

ACQUISITIONS EDITOR

Jen Cullerton Johnson writes and teaches in Chicago, Illinois. She is the author of the award-winning children's book *Seeds of Change* and the forthcoming textbook *Green Literary: Fueling Critical Conversations*. Jen is cofounder of GreenLiteracy.org, which connects environmental issues and children's literature. Her non-fiction has won several awards, including an Illinois Artist Fellowship grant. Jen earned her M.F.A. from the University of New Orleans and her M.Ed. from Loyola University of Chicago. She is at work on a middle-grade novel.

www.ingramcontent.com/pod-product-compliance
Lightning Source LLC
Chambersburg PA
CBHW030520020726
47494CB00004B/1170